Just Read!

Student Workbook

Jenn Clark and Michelle McIntosh

Just Read! Student Workbook

The authors have asserted their rights in accordance with the Copyright, Designs and Patents Act (1988) to be identified as the authors of this work.

Published by:
Pavilion Publishing and Media Ltd
Blue Sky Offices
25 Cecil Pashley Way
Shoreham by Sea
West Sussex
BN43 5FF
UK

Tel: 01273 434 943
Email: info@pavpub.com
Web: www.pavpub.com

Published 2022

A catalogue record for this book is available from the British Library.

ISBN: 978-1-913414-63-4

Pavilion Publishing and Media is a leading publisher of books, training materials and digital content in mental health, social care and allied fields. Pavilion and its imprints offer must-have knowledge and innovative learning solutions underpinned by sound research and professional values.

Authors: Jenn Clark and Michelle McIntosh
Editor: Mike Benge, Pavilion Publishing and Media
Cover design: Tony Pitt, Pavilion Publishing and Media
Page layout and typesetting: Tony Pitt, Pavilion Publishing and Media
Printing: Ashford Press

Contents

Comprehension Plus! **157**

Decoding Plus!

Rapid Letter Naming

Student

RN-1

b	F	a	G	d	e	R	y	u	O
w	Q	x	M	k	i	t	s	H	j
c	V	B	S	Y	o	U	o	P	A
f	g	L	J	h	n	z	Y	m	q
M	p	l	i	r	T	X	z	W	b
r	q	f	g	l	i	V	H	K	l
G	y	U	D	r	y	q	u	H	J
i	e	V	t	d	o	p	z	X	C
b	F	a	G	d	e	R	y	u	O
w	Q	x	M	k	i	t	s	H	j

Rapid Letter Naming

Student

RN-2

V	b	n	s	D	f	j	l	K	z
B	y	W	r	p	t	i	o	X	z
t	q	e	R	d	h	P	a	F	V
z	w	U	m	C	s	e	r	O	n
n	i	a	u	B	f	y	z	M	V
t	q	e	R	d	h	P	a	F	V
V	b	n	s	D	f	j	l	K	z
A	y	x	T	p	Q	g	H	k	L
z	w	U	m	C	s	e	r	O	n
t	q	e	R	d	h	P	a	F	V

Rapid Letter Naming

Student

RN-3

V	b	n	s	D	f	j	l	K	z
B	y	W	r	p	t	i	o	X	z
t	q	e	R	d	h	P	a	F	V
z	w	U	m	C	s	e	r	O	n
n	i	a	u	B	f	y	z	M	V
t	q	e	R	d	h	P	a	F	V
V	b	n	s	D	f	j	l	K	z
A	y	x	T	p	Q	g	H	k	L
z	w	U	m	C	s	e	r	O	n
t	q	e	R	d	h	P	a	F	V

Rapid Letter Naming

Student

RN-4

R	e	a	d	h	q	V	P	F	t
r	W	o	p	t	y	z	i	X	B
m	U	r	C	s	w	n	e	O	z
s	n	l	D	f	b	z	j	K	V
R	e	a	d	h	q	V	P	F	t
T	x	H	p	Q	y	L	g	k	A
s	n	l	D	f	b	z	j	K	V
R	e	a	d	h	q	V	P	F	t
m	U	r	C	s	w	n	e	O	z
R	e	a	d	h	q	V	P	F	t

 Clark, J & McIntosh, M. (2022) *Just Read* © Pavilion Publishing and Media Ltd 2022.

Rapid Letter Naming

Student

RN-5

W	r	p	o	z	t	i	y	B	X
U	m	C	r	n	s	e	w	z	O
e	R	d	a	V	h	P	q	t	F
x	T	p	H	L	Q	g	y	A	k
n	s	D	l	z	f	j	b	V	K
U	m	C	r	n	s	e	w	z	O
e	R	d	a	V	h	P	q	t	F
U	m	C	r	n	s	e	w	z	O
n	s	D	l	z	f	j	b	V	K

Rapid Letter Sound Identifcation

Student

RS-1

m	U	r	n	C	e	w	s	O	z
r	W	o	z	p	i	y	t	X	B
T	x	H	L	p	g	y	W	k	A
R	e	a	V	d	P	i	h	F	t
m	U	r	n	C	e	w	s	O	z
s	n	l	z	D	j	b	f	K	V
T	e	a	V	d	P	k	h	F	t
m	U	r	n	C	e	w	s	O	z
R	e	a	V	d	P	o	h	F	t
s	n	l	z	D	j	b	f	K	V

Rapid Letter Sound Identifcation

Student

RS-2

W	r	z	o	i	p	t	y	B	X
U	m	n	r	e	C	s	w	z	O
e	R	V	a	P	d	h	q	t	F
x	T	L	H	g	p	W	y	A	k
n	s	z	l	j	D	f	b	V	K
U	m	n	r	e	C	s	w	z	O
e	R	V	a	P	d	h	y	t	F
n	s	z	l	j	D	f	b	V	K
e	T	V	a	P	d	h	u	t	F
n	s	z	l	j	D	f	b	V	K

Rapid Letter Sound Identifcation

Student

RS-3

X	o	z	p	i	y	t	B	r	W
O	r	n	C	e	w	s	z	m	U
F	a	V	d	P	q	h	t	R	e
j	H	L	p	g	y	K	A	T	x
K	l	z	D	j	b	f	V	s	n
O	r	n	C	e	w	s	z	m	U
K	l	z	D	j	b	f	V	s	n
F	a	V	d	P	i	h	t	R	e
K	l	z	D	j	b	f	V	s	n
F	a	V	d	P	d	h	t	T	e

Rapid Letter Sound Identifcation

Student

RS-4

O	n	r	e	C	w	z	m	s	U
X	z	o	i	p	y	B	r	t	W
j	L	H	g	p	y	A	T	J	x
F	V	a	P	d	i	t	R	h	e
K	z	l	j	D	b	V	s	f	n
O	n	r	e	C	w	z	m	s	U
F	V	a	P	d	j	t	R	h	e
K	z	l	j	D	b	V	s	f	n
F	V	a	P	d	y	t	T	h	e
O	n	r	e	C	w	z	m	s	U

Rapid Letter Sound Identifcation

Student

RS-5

y	X	o	i	z	p	B	t	r	W
w	O	r	e	n	C	z	s	m	U
y	j	H	g	L	p	A	K	T	x
w	F	a	P	V	d	t	h	R	e
b	K	l	j	z	D	V	f	s	n
p	F	a	P	V	d	t	h	T	e
w	o	r	e	n	C	z	s	m	U
t	F	a	P	V	d	t	h	R	e
b	K	l	j	z	D	V	f	s	n
w	O	r	e	n	C	z	s	m	U

Phoneme to Phoneme Blending (ă)

Student

PBa-1

ap	ab	ak	af	ag	ak	ax	az	an	ad
am	an	ab	av	ax	az	al	ak	ag	af
ap	at	az	ax	ac	av	an	ap	ag	ak
aj	af	ap	ad	ac	av	ax	ac	aj	al
ap	ab	ak	af	ag	ak	ax	az	an	ad
aj	af	ap	ad	ac	av	ax	ac	aj	al
am	an	ab	av	ax	az	al	ak	ag	af
aj	af	ap	ad	ac	av	ax	ac	aj	al
ap	at	az	ax	ac	av	an	ap	ag	ak
ag	aj	ak	ap	ac	av	az	an	al	am

Phoneme to Phoneme Blending (ă)

Student

PBa-2

ap	at	az	ax	ac	av	an	ap	ag	ak
ap	ab	ak	af	ag	ak	ax	az	an	ad
aj	af	ap	ad	ac	av	ax	ac	aj	al
am	an	ab	av	ax	az	al	ak	ag	af
ap	at	az	ax	ac	av	an	ap	ag	ak
am	an	ab	av	ax	az	al	ak	ag	af
aj	af	ap	ad	ac	av	ax	ac	aj	al
aj	af	ap	ad	ac	av	ax	ac	aj	al
ag	aj	ak	ap	ac	av	az	an	al	am
ap	ab	ak	af	ag	ak	ax	az	an	ad

Phoneme to Phoneme Blending (ă)

Student

PBa-3

at	ax	ap	av	az	ạc	an	ag	ap	ak
ab	af	ap	ak	ak	ag	ax	an	az	ad
an	av	am	az	ab	ax	al	ag	ak	af
af	ad	aj	av	ap	ac	ax	aj	ac	al
at	ax	ap	av	az	ac	an	ag	ap	ak
af	ad	aj	av	ap	ac	ax	aj	ac	al
an	av	am	az	ab	ax	al	ag	ak	af
af	ad	aj	av	ap	ac	ax	aj	ac	al
ab	af	ap	ak	ak	ag	ax	an	az	ad
aj	ap	ag	av	ak	ac	az	al	an	am

Phoneme to Phoneme Blending (ă)

Student

PBa-4

am	an	ab	ax	al	av	af	ak	ag	az
ap	ab	ak	ag	ax	af	ad	az	an	ak
ap	at	az	ac	an	ax	ak	ap	ag	av
ap	ab	ak	ag	ax	af	ad	az	an	ak
aj	af	ap	ac	ax	ad	al	ac	aj	av
am	an	ab	ax	al	av	af	ak	ag	az
aj	af	ap	ac	ax	ad	al	ac	aj	av
ap	at	az	ac	an	ax	ak	ap	ag	av
aj	af	ap	ac	ax	ad	al	ac	aj	av
ag	aj	ak	ac	az	ap	am	an	al	av

Phoneme to Phoneme Blending (ă)

Student

PBa-5

an	am	av	ab	al	ag	af	az	ak	ax
at	ap	ax	az	an	ag	ak	av	ap	ac
ab	ap	af	ak	ax	an	ad	ak	az	ag
aj	ag	ap	ak	az	al	am	av	an	ac
af	aj	ad	ap	ax	aj	al	av	ac	ac
an	am	av	ab	al	ag	af	az	ak	ax
af	aj	ad	ap	ax	aj	al	av	ac	ac
ab	ap	af	ak	ax	an	ad	ak	az	ag
at	ap	ax	az	an	ag	ak	av	ap	ac
af	aj	ad	ap	ax	aj	al	av	ac	ac

Phoneme to Phoneme Blending (ĕ)

Student

PBe-1

et	ep	ed	ef	eg	ej	ek	el	ez	ex
em	en	eb	ec	ex	ek	el	ez	ej	eg
es	ep	et	ed	eb	ec	el	ez	ex	eg
ev	en	ez	et	em	ek	ef	ej	el	ep
em	en	eb	ec	ex	ek	el	ez	ej	eg
et	ep	ed	ef	eg	ej	ek	el	ez	ex
es	ep	et	ed	eb	ec	el	ez	ex	eg
em	en	eb	ec	ex	ek	el	ez	ej	eg
ev	en	ez	et	em	ek	ef	ej	el	ep
et	ep	ed	ef	eg	ej	ek	el	ez	ex

Clark, J & McIntosh, M. (2022) *Just Read* © Pavilion Publishing and Media Ltd 2022.

Phoneme to Phoneme Blending (ě)

Student

PBe-2

et	ed	ex	ep	ej	ef	el	ek	ez	eg
em	eb	eg	en	ek	ec	ez	el	ej	ex
ev	ez	ep	en	ek	et	ej	ef	el	em
es	et	eg	ep	ec	ed	ez	el	ex	eb
em	eb	eg	en	ek	ec	ez	el	ej	ex
et	ed	ex	ep	ej	ef	el	ek	ez	eg
es	et	eg	ep	ec	ed	ez	el	ex	eb
et	ed	ex	ep	ej	ef	el	ek	ez	eg
ev	ez	ep	en	ek	et	ej	ef	el	em
em	eb	eg	en	ek	ec	ez	el	ej	ex

Phoneme to Phoneme Blending (ĕ)

Student

PBe-3

eb	em	eg	ek	en	ec	el	ej	ez	ex
et	es	eg	ec	ep	ed	el	ex	ez	eb
eb	em	eg	ek	en	ec	el	ej	ez	ex
ez	ev	ep	ek	en	et	ef	el	ej	em
ed	et	ex	ej	ep	ef	ek	ez	el	eg
et	es	eg	ec	ep	ed	el	ex	ez	eb
ed	et	ex	ej	ep	ef	ek	ez	el	eg
eb	em	eg	ek	en	ec	el	ej	ez	ex
ez	ev	ep	ek	en	et	ef	el	ej	em
ed	et	ex	ej	ep	ef	ek	ez	el	eg

Phoneme to Phoneme Blending (ĕ)

Student

PBe-4

em	eg	ek	el	ec	en	ej	ez	eb	ex
ev	ep	ek	ef	et	en	el	ej	ez	em
em	eg	ek	el	ec	en	ej	ez	eb	ex
es	eg	ec	el	ed	ep	ex	ez	et	eb
et	ex	ej	ek	ef	ep	ez	el	ed	eg
es	eg	ec	el	ed	ep	ex	ez	et	eb
et	ex	ej	ek	ef	ep	ez	el	ed	eg
et	ex	ej	ek	ef	ep	ez	el	ed	eg
ev	ep	ek	ef	et	en	el	ej	ez	em
em	eg	ek	el	ec	en	ej	ez	eb	ex

Phoneme to Phoneme Blending (ĕ)

Student

PBe-5

ev	ek	ef	et	ep	en	el	ej	ez	em
em	ek	el	ec	eg	en	ej	ez	eb	ex
et	ej	ek	ef	ex	ep	ez	el	ed	eg
es	ec	el	ed	eg	ep	ex	ez	et	eb
em	ek	el	ec	eg	en	ej	ez	eb	ex
et	ej	ek	ef	ex	ep	ez	el	ed	eg
es	ec	el	ed	eg	ep	ex	ez	et	eb
et	ej	ek	ef	ex	ep	ez	el	ed	eg
em	ek	el	ec	eg	en	ej	ez	eb	ex
ev	ek	ef	et	ep	en	el	ej	ez	em

Phoneme to Phoneme Blending (ĭ)

Student

PBi-1

ip	it	is	id	if	ig	ij	ik	il	iz
ic	iv	ib	in	im	iz	ic	it	ip	ig
il	ij	ip	ig	iv	ik	id	ib	iz	ix
ip	it	is	id	if	ig	ij	ik	il	iz
ip	it	is	id	if	ig	ij	ik	il	iz
il	ij	ip	ig	iv	ik	id	ib	iz	ix
ip	it	is	id	if	ig	ij	ik	il	iz
ic	iv	ib	in	im	iz	ic	it	ip	ig
iv	ig	ij	ip	it	id	iz	in	ij	il
ip	it	is	id	if	ig	ij	ik	il	iz

Clark, J & McIntosh, M. (2022) *Just Read* © Pavilion Publishing and Media Ltd 2022.

Phoneme to Phoneme Blending (ĭ)

Student

PBi-2

iv	ic	ib	im	in	ic	ij	iz	it	ig
ig	iv	ij	it	ip	iz	im	id	in	il
ij	il	ip	iv	ig	id	if	ik	ib	ix
it	ip	is	if	id	ij	ix	ig	ik	iz
ig	iv	ij	it	ip	iz	im	id	in	il
it	ip	is	if	id	ij	ix	ig	ik	iz
iv	ic	ib	im	in	ic	ij	iz	it	ig
it	ip	is	if	id	ij	ix	ig	ik	iz
ig	iv	ij	it	ip	iz	im	id	in	il
ij	il	ip	iv	ig	id	if	ik	ib	ix

Phoneme to Phoneme Blending (ĭ)

Student

PBi-3

iv	ib	ic	im	ic	in	iz	ij	ig	it
ig	ij	iv	it	iz	ip	id	im	il	in
it	is	ip	if	ij	id	ig	ix	iz	ik
ij	ip	il	iv	id	ig	ik	if	ix	ib
ig	ij	iv	it	iz	ip	id	im	il	in
iv	ib	ic	im	ic	in	iz	ij	ig	it
it	is	ip	if	ij	id	ig	ix	iz	ik
it	is	ip	if	ij	id	ig	ix	iz	ik
ij	ip	il	iv	id	ig	ik	if	ix	ib
ig	ij	iv	it	iz	ip	id	im	il	in

Phoneme to Phoneme Blending (ĭ)

Student

PBi-4

ic	iv	in	it	ib	im	ij	iz	ic	ig
iz	ig	ip	in	ij	it	im	id	iv	il
ij	it	id	ik	is	if	ix	ig	ip	iz
id	ij	ig	ib	ip	iv	if	ik	il	ix
iz	ig	ip	in	ij	it	im	id	iv	il
ij	it	id	ik	is	if	ix	ig	ip	iz
ic	iv	in	it	ib	im	ij	iz	ic	ig
id	ij	ig	ib	ip	iv	if	ik	il	ix
ij	it	id	ik	is	if	ix	ig	ip	iz
iz	ig	ip	in	ij	it	im	id	iv	il

Phoneme to Phoneme Blending (ĭ)

Student

PBi-5

ig	ic	iz	iv	ib	in	im	ic	it	ij
iz	ij	ig	it	is	id	if	ip	ik	ix
il	iz	id	ig	ij	ip	it	iv	in	im
ix	id	ik	ij	ip	ig	iv	il	ib	if
iz	ij	ig	it	is	id	if	ip	ik	ix
il	iz	id	ig	ij	ip	it	iv	in	im
ig	ic	iz	iv	ib	in	im	ic	it	ij
iz	ij	ig	it	is	id	if	ip	ik	ix
ix	id	ik	ij	ip	ig	iv	il	ib	if
il	iz	id	ig	ij	ip	it	iv	in	im

Phoneme to Phoneme Blending (ŏ)

Student

PBo-1

ot	op	os	od	og	oj	ok	ol	oz	ox
ov	ob	on	om	oc	ox	oz	ol	oj	ok
ot	op	os	od	og	oj	ol	om	on	ox
ov	ob	on	ot	op	os	od	og	ol	on
oz	ok	ol	od	ob	os	og	oj	oc	ol
ov	ox	on	ot	op	os	od	og	ol	on
ot	op	os	od	og	oj	ol	om	on	ox
oz	ok	ol	od	ob	os	og	oj	oc	ol
ov	ob	on	om	oc	ox	oz	ol	oj	ok
ot	op	os	od	og	oj	ok	ol	oz	ox

Phoneme to Phoneme Blending (ŏ)

Student

PBo-2

ob	on	oc	ok	om	ol	ox	oz	ov	oj
op	os	og	ox	od	om	oj	ol	ot	on
ob	on	op	on	ot	og	os	od	ov	ol
op	os	og	ox	od	ol	oj	ok	ot	oz
ok	ol	ob	ol	od	oj	os	og	oz	oc
ox	on	op	on	ot	og	os	od	ov	ol
op	os	og	ox	od	ol	oj	ok	ot	oz
ok	ol	ob	ol	od	oj	os	og	oz	oc
op	os	og	ox	od	om	oj	ol	ot	on
ob	on	oc	ok	om	ol	ox	oz	ov	oj

Phoneme to Phoneme Blending (ŏ)

Student

PBo-3

ov	om	on	ox	oz	ob	oj	ol	ok	oc
ot	od	os	oj	ol	op	on	om	ox	og
oz	od	ol	os	og	ok	oc	oj	ol	ob
ot	od	os	oj	ok	op	oz	ol	ox	og
ov	ot	on	os	od	ox	ol	og	on	op
ot	od	os	oj	ol	op	on	om	ox	og
ov	ot	on	os	od	ob	ol	og	on	op
oz	od	ol	os	og	ok	oc	oj	ol	ob
ov	om	on	ox	oz	ob	oj	ol	ok	oc
ot	od	os	oj	ok	op	oz	ol	ox	og

Phoneme to Phoneme Blending (ŏ)

Student

PBo-4

oz	od	os	ol	ok	og	ol	oj	oc	ob
ot	od	oj	os	op	ok	ox	ol	oz	og
ov	ot	os	on	ox	od	on	og	ol	op
ot	od	oj	os	op	ol	ox	om	on	og
ov	ot	os	on	ob	od	on	og	ol	op
ot	od	oj	os	op	ok	ox	ol	oz	og
ov	om	ox	on	ob	oz	ok´	ol	oj	oc
oz	od	os	ol	ok	og	ol	oj	oc	ob
ov	om	ox	on	ob	oz	ok	ol	oj	oc
ot	od	oj	os	op	ol	ox	om	on	og

Phoneme to Phoneme Blending (ŏ)

Student

PBo-5

ol	ok	od	oz	os	ol	oc	oj	ob	og
on	ob	om	ov	ox	ok	oj	ol	oc	oz
on	ox	ot	ov	os	on	ol	og	op	od
os	op	od	ot	oj	ox	on	om	og	ol
on	ob	ot	ov	os	on	ol	og	op	od
os	op	od	ot	oj	ox	oz	ol	og	ok
on	ob	om	ov	ox	ok	oj	ol	oc	oz
os	op	od	ot	oj	ox	oz	ol	og	ok
ol	ok	od	oz	os	ol	oc	oj	ob	og
os	op	od	ot	oj	ox	on	om	og	ol

Phoneme to Phoneme Blending (ŭ)

Student

PBu-1

ut	up	us	ud	uf	ug	uj	uk	ul	uz
um	un	uv	uc	ux	uz	ul	uk	uj	ug
ud	us	up	ut	ud	uv	ub	ux	uj	uk
ut	ud	uj	uk	uc	uz	um	ub	uk	ul
uv	up	us	ud	uf	ug	uj	uk	ul	uz
um	un	uv	uc	ux	uz	ul	uk	uj	ug
ub	un	uz	up	ut	ud	ug	uk	ul	ud
ud	us	up	ut	ud	uv	ub	ux	uj	uk
uv	ud	uj	uk	uc	uz	um	ub	uk	ul
ut	up	us	ud	uf	ug	uj	uk	ul	uz

Phoneme to Phoneme Blending (ŭ)

Student

PBu-2

ud	uk	uz	uj	uc	um	uk	ub	ul	uv
un	uc	uz	uv	ux	ul	uj	uk	ug	um
us	ut	uv	up	ud	ub	uj	ux	uk	ud
up	ud	ug	us	uf	uj	ul	uk	uz	uv
un	uc	uz	uv	ux	ul	uj	uk	ug	um
ud	uk	uz	uj	uc	um	uk	ub	ul	ut
up	ud	ug	us	uf	uj	ul	uk	uz	ut
un	up	ud	uz	ut	ug	ul	uk	ud	ub
us	ut	uv	up	ud	ub	uj	ux	uk	ud
up	ud	ug	us	uf	uj	ul	uk	uz	ut

Phoneme to Phoneme Blending (ŭ)

Student

PBu-3

uc	un	uv	uz	ul	ux	uk	uj	um	ug
uk	ud	uj	uz	um	uc	ub	uk	uv	ul
ud	up	us	ug	uj	uf	uk	ul	uv	uz
ut	us	up	uv	ub	ud	ux	uj	ud	uk
uk	ud	uj	uz	um	uc	ub	uk	ut	ul
uc	un	uv	uz	ul	ux	uk	uj	um	ug
up	un	uz	ud	ug	ut	uk	ul	ub	ud
ud	up	us	ug	uj	uf	uk	ul	ut	uz
ut	us	up	uv	ub	ud	ux	uj	ud	uk
ud	up	us	ug	uj	uf	uk	ul	ut	uz

Phoneme to Phoneme Blending (ŭ)

Student

PBu-4

uk	up	ud	uf	us	uj	ug	ul	ut	uz
uk	un	uc	ux	uv	ul	uz	uj	um	ug
ux	us	ut	ud	up	ub	uv	uj	ud	uk
uk	up	ud	uf	us	uj	ug	ul	uv	uz
ub	ud	uk	uc	uj	um	uz	uk	ut	ul
uk	un	uc	ux	uv	ul	uz	uj	um	ug
uk	un	up	ut	uz	ug	ud	ul	ub	ud
ub	ud	uk	uc	uj	um	uz	uk	uv	ul
ux	us	ut	ud	up	ub	uv	uj	ud	uk
uk	up	ud	uf	us	uj	ug	ul	ut	uz

Phoneme to Phoneme Blending (ŭ)

Student

PBu-5

ul	uc	un	ux	ul	uv	uz	um	uj	ug
um	ud	up	uf	uj	us	ug	uv	ul	uz
ux	ut	us	ud	ub	up	uv	ud	uj	uk
ub	uk	ud	uc	um	uj	uz	ut	uk	ul
uk	ud	up	uf	uj	us	ug	ut	ul	uz
uf	uc	un	ux	ul	uv	uz	um	uj	ug
ub	uk	ud	uc	um	uj	uz	uv	uk	ul
uk	up	un	ut	ug	uz	ud	ub	ul	ud
ux	ut	us	ud	ub	up	uv	ud	uj	uk
uj	ud	up	uf	uj	us	ug	ut	ul	uz

Phoneme to Phoneme Blending (Mixed)

Student

PBm-1

av	et	ut	ob	ek	iv	og	id	af	oc
ib	um	ol	ad	ev	ex	ic	ok	al	ov
ig	ud	ej	ox	iv	ap	ub	ik	os	ec
of	es	id	eg	av	ak	uz	ix	ap	od
am	on	eb	ud	iz	ux	at	im	op	ix
ab	og	uz	om	it	ec	il	ox	ez	uf
ig	uj	az	ov	eb	im	ux	oz	ac	ol
el	uk	in	ez	oj	aj	ib	ov	ep	iz
ol	ug	ij	ak	ec	ud	oc	iv	ag	ef
ob	ig	ap	ed	ux	ev	ib	od	uz	ik

Phoneme to Phoneme Blending (Mixed)

Student

PBm-2

um	ib	ad	ol	ex	ev	ok	ic	ov	al
et	av	ob	ut	iv	ek	id	og	oc	af
es	of	eg	id	ak	av	ix	uz	od	ap
ud	ig	ox	ej	ap	iv	ik	ub	ec	os
og	ab	om	uz	ec	it	ox	il	uf	ez
on	am	ud	eb	ux	iz	im	at	ix	op
uk	el	ez	in	aj	oj	ov	ib	iz	ep
uj	ig	ov	az	im	eb	oz	ux	ol	ac
ig	ob	ed	ap	ev	ux	od	ib	ik	uz
ug	ol	ak	ij	ud	ec	iv	oc	ef	ag

Phoneme to Phoneme Blending (Mixed)

Student

PBm-3

av	et	ob	iv	ut	id	ek	og	af	oc
ib	um	ad	ex	ol	ok	ev	ic	al	ov
ig	ud	ox	ap	ej	ik	iv	ub	os	ec
of	es	eg	ak	id	ix	av	uz	ap	od
ab	og	om	ec	uz	ox	it	il	ez	uf
el	uk	ez	aj	in	ov	oj	ib	ep	iz
am	on	ud	ux	eb	im	iz	at	op	ix
ob	ig	ed	ev	ap	od	ux	ib	uz	ik
ig	uj	ov	im	az	oz	eb	ux	ac	ol
ol	ug	ak	ud	ij	iv	ec	oc	ag	ef

 Clark, J & McIntosh, M. (2022) *Just Read* © Pavilion Publishing and Media Ltd 2022.

Phoneme to Phoneme Blending (Mixed)

Student

PBm-4

ol	ib	ad	um	ex	ok	ic	ev	ov	al
id	of	eg	es	ak	ix	uz	av	od	ap
az	ig	ov	uj	im	oz	ux	eb	ol	ac
ej	ig	ox	ud	ap	ik	ub	iv	ec	os
uz	ab	om	og	ec	ox	il	it	uf	ez
in	el	ez	uk	aj	ov	ib	oj	iz	ep
eb	am	ud	on	ux	im	at	iz	ix	op
ij	ol	ak	ug	ud	iv	oc	ec	ef	ag
ap	ob	ed	ig	ev	od	ib	ux	ik	uz
ut	av	ob	et	iv	id	og	ek	oc	af

Phoneme to Phoneme Blending (Mixed)

Student

PBm-5

of	id	eg	ak	ix	av	es	uz	ap	od
av	ut	ob	iv	id	ek	et	og	af	oc
ig	ej	ox	ap	ik	iv	ud	ub	os	ec
ab	uz	om	ec	ox	it	og	il	ez	uf
el	in	ez	aj	ov	oj	uk	ib	ep	iz
ig	az	ov	im	oz	eb	uj	ux	ac	ol
am	eb	ud	ux	im	iz	on	at	op	ix
ol	ij	ak	ud	iv	ec	ug	oc	ag	ef
ob	ap	ed	ev	od	ux	ig	ib	uz	ik
ib	ol	ad	ex	ok	ev	um	ic	al	ov

Pseudo-Word (CVC) Reading (ă)

Student

PSWa-1

bap	caf	gat	mak	pab	jad	mab	laj	zak	hax
baz	dag	maj	vap	zat	sav	rax	lav	taj	wam
jat	lan	waj	vax	naf	faz	gan	lak	pav	zad
hab	jal	cax	yan	vad	gad	waz	paj	kak	mal
raf	yax	hal	nan	cav	bab	rav	gat	haf	laz
das	wab	yad	kax	nas	dac	bap	baf	nam	ral
san	mas	fam	hac	kal	laz	baj	dab	vaz	dag
wad	fab	jac	pag	raf	wat	gax	san	tak	cam
zat	baz	paz	jan	bac	gat	hac	gad	raz	daf
sab	fac	dax	paz	vam	pag	sab	kak	cav	gam

Pseudo-Word (CVC) Reading (ă)

Student

PSWa-2

baz	wam	maj	dag	zat	vap	rax	sav	taj	lav
bap	hax	gat	caf	pab	mak	mab	jad	zak	laj
hab	mal	cax	jal	vad	yan	waz	gad	kak	paj
jat	zad	waj	lan	naf	vax	gan	faz	pav	lak
das	ral	yad	wab	nas	kax	bap	dac	nam	baf
raf	laz	hal	yax	cav	nan	rav	bab	haf	gat
san	dag	fam	mas	kal	hac	baj	laz	vaz	dab
zat	daf	paz	baz	bac	jan	hac	gat	raz	gad
wad	cam	jac	fab	raf	pag	gax	wat	tak	san
sab	gam	dax	fac	vam	paz	sab	pag	cav	kak

 Clark, J & McIntosh, M. (2022) *Just Read* © Pavilion Publishing and Media Ltd 2022.

Pseudo-Word (CVC) Reading (ă)

Student

PSWa-3

pab	bap	gat	hax	caf	mab	jad	mak	laj	zak
vad	hab	cax	mal	jal	waz	gad	yan	paj	kak
zat	baz	maj	wam	dag	rax	sav	vap	lav	taj
naf	jat	waj	zad	lan	gan	faz	vax	lak	pav
nas	das	yad	ral	wab	bap	dac	kax	baf	nam
vam	sab	dax	gam	fac	sab	pag	paz	kak	cav
cav	raf	hal	laz	yax	rav	bab	nan	gat	haf
kal	san	fam	dag	mas	baj	laz	hac	dab	vaz
raf	wad	jac	cam	fab	gax	wat	pag	san	tak
bac	zat	paz	daf	baz	hac	gat	jan	gad	raz

Pseudo-Word (CVC) Reading (ă)

Student

PSWa-4

raf	hac	mab	bap	laf	maz	zab	rax	pac	cav
zad	daf	gan	pak	yax	jaf	pap	laz	mam	nad
lal	baf	fac	laj	jax	wad	mag	gad	bab	dag
haz	zaj	dax	wak	mak	rab	wab	maf	faj	jat
dap	wav	lak	dag	zaf	hab	rab	tac	mak	dav
lat	bav	rab	bap	kat	naj	vab	wap	sab	baf
nac	dac	waz	jak	pak	sab	mag	baj	wav	caz
paj	lav	raj	rax	nad	waj	vaf	faz	mak	lac
tam	jax	cav	jaj	lan	nan	waf	paj	laz	tav
vab	ral	caj	vab	saf	pas	mam	jad	sas	yab

Pseudo-Word (CVC) Reading (ă)

Student

PSWa-5

hac	zab	bap	laf	mab	maz	raf	cav	rax	pac
jax	waf	jaj	lan	cav	nan	tam	tav	paj	laz
baf	mag	laj	jax	fac	wad	lal	dag	gad	bab
wav	rab	dag	zaf	lak	hab	dap	dav	tac	mak
zaj	wab	wak	mak	dax	rab	haz	jat	maf	faj
daf	pap	pak	yax	gan	jaf	zad	nad	laz	mam
bav	vab	bap	kat	rab	naj	lat	baf	wap	sab
dac	mag	jak	pak	waz	sab	nac	caz	baj	wav
lav	vaf	rax	nad	raj	waj	paj	lac	faz	mak
ral	mam	vab	saf	caj	pas	vab	yab	jad	sas

Pseudo-Word (CVC) Reading (ĕ)

Student

PSWe-1

fek	yed	tev	pex	yev	bes	seb	jep	pef	fen
mez	ket	lec	ven	nen	hez	lep	pel	rel	tex
ved	mez	neb	beb	jek	dej	jeb	pev	jez	nef
yez	mev	lex	kek	lev	mes	sep	heb	bef	leb
wec	reb	tez	yej	pec	sef	deg	fek	hev	jex
kev	lep	zeg	ved	bex	nej	mef	fef	zec	seb
mez	nex	yed	jef	pej	vev	hep	dek	fex	zep
yem	jez	les	reg	tep	jej	nep	zes	ved	lex
tef	yek	pec	sez	dex	fev	heb	jed	rel	weg
mev	nep	zev	bek	ved	mem	pel	hev	kem	lep

 Clark, J & McIntosh, M. (2022) *Just Read* © Pavilion Publishing and Media Ltd 2022.

Pseudo-Word (CVC) Reading (ĕ)

Student

PSWe-2

ket	mez	ven	lec	hez	nen	pel	lep	tex	rel
yed	fek	pex	tev	bes	yev	jep	seb	fen	pef
mev	yez	kek	lex	mes	lev	heb	sep	leb	bef
mez	ved	beb	neb	dej	jek	pev	jeb	nef	jez
lep	kev	ved	zeg	nej	bex	fef	mef	seb	zec
reb	wec	yej	tez	sef	pec	fek	deg	jex	hev
jez	yem	reg	les	jej	tep	zes	nep	lex	ved
nex	mez	jef	yed	vev	pej	dek	hep	zep	fex
nep	mev	bek	zev	mem	ved	hev	pel	lep	kem
yek	tef	sez	pec	fev	dex	jed	heb	weg	rel

Pseudo-Word (CVC) Reading (ĕ)

Student

PSWe-3

fek	yed	tev	feg	kev	wef	rep	weg	jem	ken
wep	rep	tef	bep	tej	pes	kep	reb	sep	rez
bev	deg	reb	dev	pem	bec	zet	feg	pej	reg
kel	jep	rep	sez	pek	sed	pem	meg	wez	leb
deg	zed	heb	nes	fep	det	feg	sev	peb	hed
kes	jek	pef	fec	bef	ket	yev	nen	wes	jeg
ved	sez	kef	zep	feg	lem	mex	hev	nev	wep
bex	mep	ped	het	yex	zes	ved	jel	bej	wec
lrp	mem	pex	lef	fet	veg	hek	lep	mez	zej
jev	nef	mez	pek	tev	beb	kem	jex	keb	feb

Pseudo-Word (CVC) Reading (ě)

Student

PSWe-4

nef	pek	beb	tev	jex	keb	kem	mez	feb	jev
yed	feg	wef	kev	weg	jem	rep	tev	ken	fek
deg	dev	bec	pem	feg	pej	zet	reb	reg	bev
jep	sez	sed	pek	meg	wez	pem	rep	leb	kel
rep	bep	pes	tej	reb	sep	kep	tef	rez	wep
zed	nes	det	fep	sev	peb	feg	heb	hed	deg
mem	lef	veg	fet	lep	mez	hek	pex	zej	lrp
jek	fec	ket	bef	nen	wes	yev	pef	jeg	kes
mep	het	zes	yex	jel	bej	ved	ped	wec	bex
sez	zep	lem	feg	hev	nev	mex	kef	wep	ved

Pseudo-Word (CVC) Reading (ĕ)

Student

PSWe-5

feg	yed	kev	wef	jem	weg	tev	rep	fek	ken
pek	nef	tev	beb	keb	jex	mez	kem	jev	feb
sez	jep	pek	sed	wez	meg	rep	pem	kel	leb
dev	deg	pem	bec	pej	feg	reb	zet	bev	reg
nes	zed	fep	det	peb	sev	heb	feg	deg	hed
bep	rep	tej	pes	sep	reb	tef	kep	wep	rez
fec	jek	bef	ket	wes	nen	pef	yev	kes	jeg
lef	mem	fet	veg	mez	lep	pex	hek	lrp	zej
zep	sez	feg	lem	nev	hev	kef	mex	ved	wep
het	mep	yex	zes	bej	jel	ped	ved	bex	wec

Pseudo-Word (CVC) Reading (ĭ)

Student

PSWi-1

pip	lim	nip	pim	fiv	vid	diz	vix	kib	bik
mim	nid	dit	tig	hif	fip	sid	wip	tib	lis
sib	vin	pix	rij	kix	bis	wiz	rif	tik	yix
piz	sij	div	fim	hic	jik	kiv	liz	zib	viv
bip	nix	mif	wix	rij	tiv	yip	nin	kij	jix
mij	lig	hib	biv	ziv	dil	fid	wik	yit	vit
fif	jiv	wip	jix	mil	kiv	rix	miz	bij	dif
sib	nif	kij	mig	vib	zig	hiv	pik	liv	dil
hib	fiv	nig	jil	ziz	sig	nix	vig	bix	rif
lib	bip	siz	hix	kib	dil	liz	hij	piv	rix

Pseudo-Word (CVC) Reading (ĭ)

Student

PSWi-2

fiv	vid	diz	pim	lim	vix	kib	nip	bik	pip
kix	bis	wiz	rij	vin	rif	tik	pix	yix	sib
hic	jik	kiv	fim	sij	liz	zib	div	viv	piz
rij	tiv	yip	wix	nix	nin	kij	mif	jix	bip
hif	fip	sid	tig	nid	wip	tib	dit	lis	mim
ziv	dil	fid	biv	lig	wik	yit	hib	vit	mij
kib	dil	liz	hix	bip	hij	piv	siz	rix	lib
mil	kiv	rix	jix	jiv	miz	bij	wip	dif	fif
vib	zig	hiv	mig	nif	pik	liv	kij	dil	sib
ziz	sig	nix	jil	fiv	vig	bix	nig	rif	hib

Pseudo-Word (CVC) Reading (ĭ)

Student

PSWi-3

ziz	nix	sig	fiv	jil	bix	vig	nig	hib	rif
hic	kiv	jik	sij	fim	zib	liz	div	piz	viv
kix	wiz	bis	vin	rij	tik	rif	pix	sib	yix
hif	sid	fip	nid	tig	tib	wip	dit	mim	lis
ziv	fid	dil	lig	biv	yit	wik	hib	mij	vit
rij	yip	tiv	nix	wix	kij	nin	mif	bip	jix
kib	liz	dil	bip	hix	piv	hij	siz	lib	rix
vib	hiv	zig	nif	mig	liv	pik	kij	sib	dil
mil	rix	kiv	jiv	jix	bij	miz	wip	fif	dif
fiv	diz	vid	lim	pim	kib	vix	nip	pip	bik

Clark, J & McIntosh, M. (2022) *Just Read* © Pavilion Publishing and Media Ltd 2022.

Pseudo-Word (CVC) Reading (ĭ)

Student

PSWi-4

jig	pik	hif	vix	lif	pib	viz	lin	kiv	lig
bim	tiv	kij	pif	biv	tic	div	sid	dix	piv
jik	liz	dib	bik	piz	fip	miz	fip	zin	miv
vig	hib	nif	mip	pik	kib	vip	zid	sid	wib
vib	sif	fid	diz	hij	jix	ric	nig	kiz	vip
mim	pij	lig	tib	bis	div	vid	zij	bim	pip
zix	pib	kij	jiv	div	hix	mip	piz	yim	vit
tid	fid	sij	fik	lif	ris	liz	hix	biv	wip
rix	kif	lij	zig	hiv	jik	kib	liz	pib	bif
hig	jip	bix	niv	zid	kif	sib	tiz	lif	pif

 Clark, J & McIntosh, M. (2022) *Just Read* © Pavilion Publishing and Media Ltd 2022.

Pseudo-Word (CVC) Reading (ĭ)

Student

PSWi-5

vig	hib	mip	pik	zid	kib	vip	wib	sid	nif
mim	pij	tib	bis	zij	div	vid	pip	bim	lig
vib	sif	diz	hij	nig	jix	ric	vip	kiz	fid
zix	pib	jiv	div	piz	hix	mip	vit	yim	kij
tid	fid	fik	lif	hix	ris	liz	wip	biv	sij
jik	liz	bik	piz	fip	fip	miz	miv	zin	dib
rix	kif	zig	hiv	liz	jik	kib	bif	pib	lij
bim	tiv	pif	biv	sid	tic	div	piv	dix	kij
hig	jip	niv	zid	tiz	kif	sib	pif	lif	bix
jig	pik	vix	lif	lin	pib	viz	lig	kiv	hif

Pseudo-Word (CVC) Reading (ŏ)

Student

PSWo-1

wob	rov	tox	wol	yob	poz	sov	dox	fon	goj
hoz	jop	cos	lod	zon	coj	vop	lol	bom	nop
wof	hol	rop	bol	tob	yog	pog	sox	dob	fov
gov	hox	joz	lod	zob	cof	vom	bop	nof	mox
wov	rog	tod	yoz	pos	sov	doc	tol	fof	yot
yom	mol	pob	soz	dod	fop	gof	nol	hod	nop
mon	bol	yop	vog	hon	lod	zoz	jox	fot	jok
rov	bok	dof	gog	fod	sov	cos	loz	fos	lon
gop	fod	jod	mog	coz	nop	pok	doz	rox	bov
dop	foj	rol	vod	yov	zol	tof	moj	dop	bok

Pseudo-Word (CVC) Reading (ŏ)

Student

PSWo-2

jop	hoz	lod	cos	coj	zon	lol	vop	nop	bom
rov	wob	wol	tox	poz	yob	dox	sov	goj	fon
hox	gov	lod	joz	cof	zob	bop	vom	mox	nof
hol	wof	bol	rop	yog	tob	sox	pog	fov	dob
mol	yom	soz	pob	fop	dod	nol	gof	nop	hod
rog	wov	yoz	tod	sov	pos	tol	doc	yot	fof
bok	rov	gog	dof	sov	fod	loz	cos	lon	fos
bol	mon	vog	yop	lod	hon	jox	zoz	jok	fot
foj	dop	vod	rol	zol	yov	moj	tof	bok	dop
fod	gop	mog	jod	nop	coz	doz	pok	bov	rox

Pseudo-Word (CVC) Reading (ŏ)

Student

PSWo-3

gop	pok	mog	rox	jod	nop	coz	doz	bov	fod
gov	vom	lod	nof	joz	cof	zob	bop	mox	hox
wof	pog	bol	dob	rop	yog	tob	sox	fov	hol
wob	sov	wol	fon	tox	poz	yob	dox	goj	rov
yom	gof	soz	hod	pob	fop	dod	nol	nop	mol
wov	doc	yoz	fof	tod	sov	pos	tol	yot	rog
rov	cos	gog	fos	dof	sov	fod	loz	lon	bok
mon	zoz	vog	fot	yop	lod	hon	jox	jok	bol
hoz	vop	lod	bom	cos	coj	zon	lol	nop	jop
dop	tof	vod	foj	rol	zol	yov	moj	bok	foj

Pseudo-Word (CVC) Reading (ŏ)

Student

PSWo-4

poc	hos	gob	rof	pok	roz	zot	dop	toz	wob
tod	wof	fot	lok	rog	poc	lom	mog	wok	pog
loj	sog	mox	dob	com	roz	fov	vox	jom	lov
zop	mov	pon	hoj	lok	mox	cof	fos	woj	jon
cov	bom	yod	jol	poj	hox	vov	zok	los	wof
pof	yog	vob	zoz	hon	pok	sop	jox	dop	bos
los	fot	boz	coj	wov	nof	gox	roj	lok	sov
yox	woz	rop	tob	pon	sof	dov	foz	gog	hok
joc	loz	zop	cof	vod	bol	nok	mov	wox	roj
toc	yod	pol	sov	dox	fov	gom	hos	jol	loc

Pseudo-Word (CVC) Reading (ŏ)

Student

PSWo-5

pok	hos	rof	roz	zot	poc	dop	wob	toz	gob
rog	wof	lok	poc	lom	tod	mog	pog	wok	fot
lok	mov	hoj	mox	cof	zop	fos	jon	woj	pon
poj	bom	jol	hox	vov	cov	zok	wof	los	yod
dox	yod	sov	fov	gom	toc	hos	loc	jol	pol
com	sog	dob	roz	fov	loj	vox	lov	jom	mox
hon	yog	zoz	pok	sop	pof	jox	bos	dop	vob
wov	fot	coj	nof	gox	los	roj	sov	lok	boz
vod	loz	cof	bol	nok	joc	mov	roj	wox	zop
pon	woz	tob	sof	dov	yox	foz	hok	gog	rop

 Clark, J & McIntosh, M. (2022) *Just Read* © Pavilion Publishing and Media Ltd 2022.

Pseudo-Word (CVC) Reading (ŭ)

Student

PSWu-1

wup	ruv	tuc	yun	puz	sup	duc	fub	gug	jup
lud	suz	zub	cun	vuf	bup	nud	mus	wul	ruc
yud	puj	sug	duf	fuv	guc	hux	jus	lup	zuz
cuf	vud	buj	nup	muf	rul	tun	yud	puc	sux
duf	fuz	gup	huv	jum	luz	zug	cul	vum	bup
wul	rup	yut	tut	pux	suj	duk	fuv	gul	huz
bux	wun	ruf	tuv	yud	pux	sut	duz	fub	gup
huc	jun	lup	zuv	cux	vud	buj	nup	mut	wub
lup	rux	yud	pud	fuf	gud	huc	jub	luz	zup
mun	bup	wud	zuz	pum	juf	fut	zux	sup	nug

Pseudo-Word (CVC) Reading (ŭ)

Student

PSWu-2

ruv	wup	tuc	puz	yun	sup	fub	duc	jup	gug
puj	yud	sug	fuv	duf	guc	jus	hux	zuz	lup
suz	lud	zub	vuf	cun	bup	mus	nud	ruc	wul
fuz	duf	gup	jum	huv	luz	cul	zug	bup	vum
vud	cuf	buj	muf	nup	rul	yud	tun	sux	puc
wun	bux	ruf	yud	tuv	pux	duz	sut	gup	fub
rup	wul	yut	pux	tut	suj	fuv	duk	huz	gul
rux	lup	yud	fuf	pud	gud	jub	huc	zup	luz
jun	huc	lup	cux	zuv	vud	nup	buj	wub	mut
bup	mun	wud	pum	zuz	juf	zux	fut	nug	sup

Pseudo-Word (CVC) Reading (ŭ)

Student

PSWu-3

wut	rud	wup	tud	gub	nug	luz	cuz	juv	sux
yud	bux	zub	num	mux	sut	vum	nuv	puj	luk
zup	vux	huf	gup	yub	rul	lup	huv	mup	suz
puj	lun	wug	hux	zuk	sul	guv	ruf	fup	gug
zub	buv	wud	yug	gud	fug	nup	pud	dut	nuz
jud	suz	bux	vud	lup	ruj	nul	juv	muz	yux
tuv	wup	zum	mub	jun	mux	vub	rup	suz	tun
pux	buv	sus	hux	yub	nud	luz	huf	bub	yub
duf	jun	muv	yun	nug	dup	jub	lum	nux	wuv
buz	lub	wud	zuj	bub	dux	jud	sug	lum	mup

Pseudo-Word (CVC) Reading (ŭ)

Student

PSWu-4

cun	nud	mus	jus	lup	fuv	zub	suz	ruc	puj
yun	duc	fub	fub	gug	puz	wup	ruv	jup	juv
duf	hux	jus	mus	wul	vuf	huf	puj	zuz	mup
huv	zug	cul	yud	puc	muf	wud	fuz	bup	dut
nup	tun	yud	cul	vum	jum	wug	vud	sux	fup
tut	duk	fuv	duz	fub	yud	bux	rup	huz	muz
zuv	buj	nup	jub	luz	fuf	sus	jun	wub	bub
tuv	sut	duz	fuv	gul	pux	zum	wun	gup	suz
zuz	fut	zux	zux	sup	pum	wud	bup	nug	lum
pud	huc	jub	nup	mut	cux	muv	rux	zup	nux

Pseudo-Word (CVC) Reading (ŭ)

Student

PSWu-5

yud	puz	zub	cun	sut	yub	guc	mux	juv	jup
wut	fuv	tuc	yun	nug	wup	sup	gub	puj	ruc
zup	vuf	sug	duf	rul	lud	bup	yub	mup	zuz
puj	muf	buj	nup	sul	duf	luz	zuk	dut	bup
zub	jum	gup	huv	fug	cuf	rul	gud	fup	sux
tuv	fuf	ruf	tuv	mux	wul	suj	jun	bub	wub
jud	yud	yut	tut	ruj	bux	pux	lup	muz	huz
pux	pux	lup	zuv	nud	lup	gud	yub	suz	gup
buz	cux	wud	zuz	dux	mun	juf	bub	nux	zup
duf	pum	yud	pud	dup	huc	vud	nug	lum	nug

Real Word (CVC) Reading (Mixed Vowels)

Student

RWm-1

got	egg	hug	dib	dip	met	con	big	fed	hen
bid	don	did	cod	bed	cog	cot	cad	cud	bus
bin	bit	dig	din	fun	dud	gut	dim	dug	hut
dot	leg	beg	Ben	bet	den	cub	get	fab	Ed
fog	hit	bad	Ken	hip	jet	god	men	med	cut
fob	fox	fig	dog	gob	fin	his	him	hog	fit
Gus	gun	bot	bog	hub	jut	Bob	cob	cop	box
hid	gig	yap	fib	gal	wax	bat	dam	fan	bam
bam	can	bag	dad	cap	ban	dab	cab	cat	fat
led	hex	bug	bun	Ned	bud	Meg	cup	but	bum

 Clark, J & McIntosh, M. (2022) *Just Read* © Pavilion Publishing and Media Ltd 2022.

Real Word (CVC) Reading (Mixed Vowels)

Student

RWm-2

had	lop	hap	gag	lax	hop	set	lox	hag	ham
lob	mid	pub	gab	fax	lap	reg	fad	gas	gap
hot	jug	job	lip	lug	mud	sit	mix	pug	sun
jog	jot	jig	kit	kid	log	lid	lot	lit	kin
mum	rug	mug	mutt	pup	nut	rum	pun	hem	pod
run	lam	sum	mob	wed	sub	non	nod	ref	ten
mod	web	nip	nib	bib	red	Zen	nix	pit	pep
nil	peg	pig	pet	pin	net	rip	rib	pen	rep
mom	vet	mop	Ted	nog	not	hog	wet	yes	yen
had	lop	hap	gag	lax	hop	set	lox	hag	ham

Real Word (CVC) Reading (Mixed Vowels)

Student

RWm-3

bin	egg	tot	win	sip	men	lax	Ned	jet	get
sit	cud	hen	rod	fed	med	tin	mad	leg	nab
man	hex	sin	sit	six	led	pun	jab	tix	lag
wig	zig	rob	fix	bug	but	rot	cub	sod	bud
nap	nag	pad	pub	nun	rig	rug	rim	rid	tip
mag	mat	map	max	tug	yum	nub	hum	gum	hub
Ken	hat	has	met	lad	Meg	lab	lam	jam	lap
pom	Tim	Sid	pot	win	pop	zip	pox	Ron	sob
bum	beg	bed	bet	cut	Ben	odd	gob	den	Ed
sog	bun	tog	bus	cup	top	ox	tom	sop	tot

Real Word (CVC) Reading (Mixed Vowels)

Student

RWm-4

rap	ten	sag	ram	ran	cup	sod	pom	tin	gig
cog	bot	lug	him	red	met	but	jug	pug	sap
hip	his	fit	leg	med	six	cot	hex	jet	Ned
box	fig	van	sob	cod	cop	hid	fin	fib	hit
pub	bum	bun	mum	pan	rad	pal	cut	rag	sad
pox	Bob	tad	rob	Ron	bog	tax	vat	con	cob
Ken	men	led	rid	rim	Meg	sit	sip	rep	ref
rig	sin	pen	net	peg	pep	tip	pet	tix	set
pot	pop	sat	sax	rod	tag	rot	tan	tap	tab
mud	nut	mug	bud	mutt	bus	pun	cub	cud	bug

Real Word (CVC) Reading (Mixed Vowels)

Student

RWm-5

vat	hex	led	got	tin	jet	men	fab	hog	tix
Meg	sip	sun	med	rut	pod	sun	run	pup	fat
sum	dog	dot	sit	gob	fox	tad	tap	fog	hog
rut	rug	dad	tub	rid	sin	rig	rim	six	tip
don	sat	fob	god	tag	tan	tab	sax	tax	van
rub	rum	sub	cad	cat	can	cap	dab	dam	fan
met	Ken	kid	leg	sit	lip	mid	Ned	jig	lit
kin	kit	pup	lid	rub	mix	sum	mop	wet	run
rum	rug	vet	Ted	hem	sub	yen	tub	non	not
web	mod	wed	Zen	mom	yes	reg	mob	nog	nod

Real Word Reading (Initial & Final Blends)

Student

RWblm-1

pond	slump	step	camp	frost	slum	went	stamp	glass	fast
swift	truck	wept	grand	fled	soft	crisp	plum	test	blunt
frog	vast	stand	blot	sand	drop	print	belt	cram	grin
rest	drift	skin	jump	stunt	trot	mist	frost	sled	weld
tramp	clock	silk	slant	cross	risk	plump	stop	bond	flint
grip	golf	brisk	bran	land	grunt	flop	lost	blend	stem
fond	scamp	grab	ramp	trust	smog	list	clump	still	help
stilt	track	desk	gland	flap	nest	flask	snip	limp	brand
smug	melt	strict	plan	bend	graft	plan	past	skimp	trick
tent	grant	bled	damp	plug	bland	lend	slip	draft	drill

Real Word Reading (Initial & Final Blends)

Student

RWblm-2

mint	trap	blimp	bent	stuff	glint	vest	black	trump	felt
flag	scalp	held	spin	crust	sent	drum	spent	west	glad
blast	lamp	brag	frisk	ant	cliff	plant	dust	grim	swept
bump	stick	twist	vent	snag	grasp	yelp	frill	squint	hand
flip	swept	dent	trim	strand	welt	spell	clasp	mast	plus
splint	black	cram	drab	flip	grub	lump	mast	welt	bend
grand	plus	scrap	wind	just	splint	blunt	lend	dump	pest
lift	quest	melt	went	swift	lint	held	plump	flask	send
cast	hump	primp	clasp	spot	grunt	snap	felt	tusk	grump
plop	gulp	raft	floss	desk	frock	blimp	rant	task	drip

Real Word Reading (Initial & Final Blends)

Student

RWblm-3

ramp	bond	blog	risk	pelt	crab	jest	clam	crust	husk
band	strand	gust	flask	past	vest	trim	scalp	blond	last
smug	fast	plod	dusk	primp	loft	clasp	melt	grim	trot
scrimp	clack	squid	twig	nest	drag	spend	brag	punt	frisk
ramp	crisp	crag	bland	flux	clamp	stub	pump	bust	vend
fret	glug	flint	hunt	slept	twin	mint	bond	swim	twin
stop	blend	grasp	must	bent	font	gland	help	just	milk
plant	splot	yelp	draft	flock	jump	trust	skip	fled	weld
mast	drip	rasp	skit	melt	trod	gloss	stump	land	test
grim	rest	drag	stomp	flat	left	glad	went	mask	best

Real Word Reading (Initial & Final Blends)

Student

RWblm-4

clump	grand	mast	still	moss	drip	grub	brand	drip	clog
drug	help	twin	brisk	just	lump	primp	flint	vast	kept
grab	bless	clog	melt	swig	kelp	scrap	strip	prod	clamp
blend	flat	grab	silt	drug	kilt	crust	hand	brick	plant
lamp	mend	belt	risk	step	pram	glint	scalp	strand	swift
smug	trick	plum	frog	cliff	drum	flap	brand	skin	black
lisp	jump	blunt	blimp	graft	slant	list	soft	limp	help
vest	bust	fond	bluff	quell	stunt	grant	slept	swill	slum
trust	glass	spell	grass	blast	plug	glad	smog	snag	slip
just	crop	wept	lump	cuff	crag	twig	west	slid	desk

Real Word Reading (Initial & Final Blends)

Student

RWblm-5

jest	clap	flan	Clem	glib	plot	glen	sled	scab	crib
drab	brat	glint	punt	print	rust	cusp	blimp	fend	gland
frump	brisk	sniff	flax	mint	brass	skill	crest	truss	scrimp
gift	dress	kilt	rapt	sect	hilt	sculpt	cleft	cull	wilt
scrub	nest	bulk	snuff	flick	track	plop	crack	tuft	gulp
sulk	cram	prod	spend	trust	smelt	trap	plug	lisp	heft
twin	crop	just	brisk	clasp	gulf	risk	text	mask	slack
welt	stress	slick	drop	drab	hemp	brag	sprat	meld	tram
swill	jest	pulp	glom	rest	vast	struck	kelp	still	stomp
wisp	fund	flop	crept	welp	flux	rift	tempt	bond	stack

Fluency Passages (CVC)

Decoding Story 1.1: "Ned the Cop"

Section 1

Isolated Phonogram Reading

c	n	s	f	p
a	b	l	e	u
t	h	s	a	b
d	i	e	o	g
j	u	k	v	d

Nonsense Word Reading

deb	cag	hep	tiv	jux
loz	yem	mif	guv	kib
nis	wep	pid	boj	nem
saf	pag	sav	mag	lig
wug	pob	suz	zib	nop

Real Word Reading

wed	cop	van	jut	not
cab	bad	run	lid	met
did	bet	pad	job	lap
pal	rob	him	mug	set
fed	top	lad	pug	leg

Decoding Story 1.1: "Ned the Cop"

Section 2

Non-phonetic Word Recognition

Only read the real words in these paragraphs.

Fex con tup are git to pex the tup
You fip feb was un kib med two fis
One paf lix rit the kiz
Oh weg coz of lil the yop

Hep one to lin qop to tup You won
feb Pon feb vit are fis des fow
Lix was you Qop sig tyop
Sav lig yen the gim saf cag

Was gim gol fop dit ros
Bab biz two you was
Kijvhiy rop the dup cirt
Nis dupol waz cuvit oh

pid hyu thi pol iy tyim
Guv mag xot em lit
hep tiw you nit ruy il
mif qep nis los zit nop

vol pliy rplo afplooi dit
one are hiplo yilk hlop
sav zin bviuy kib molk
poki mif hust ghuop ir

 Clark, J & McIntosh, M. (2022) *Just Read* © Pavilion Publishing and Media Ltd 2022.

Decoding Story 1.1: "Ned the Cop"

Section 3

Sentence Stacks

Ned was sad

Ned was sad at his

Ned was sad at his pal Sam.

Ned and Sam

Ned and Sam sat in

Ned and Sam sat in the van.

Ned had to run

Ned had to run to the cab

Ned had to run to the cab to get Sam.

Ten men met Sam

Ten men met Sam and led him

Ten men met Sam and led him to the pen.

Decoding Story 1.1: "Ned the Cop"

Section 4

Ned was a cop. Ned had fun as a cop. Ned had one pal. His pal was Sam. Sam was not a cop. Sam was a bad man on the run. Sam did rob one man. Ned was sad at his pal Sam. Sam had a bad rap. Ned had to nab his pal Sam. Ned the cop was on the job. Ned had to run to the cab to get Sam. Ned did nab Sam. Sam was too sad. His pal Ned did get him. Ned and Sam sat in the van. Ten men met Sam and led him to the pen. Ned had a mad pal. Ned was a sad lad.

 Clark, J & McIntosh, M. (2022) *Just Read* © Pavilion Publishing and Media Ltd 2022.

Decoding Story 1.2: "Flip and Flop"

Section 1

Isolated Phonogram Reading

bl	a	gl	u	fl
n	d	g	w	p
fl	l	t	g	e
o	i	pl	cl	h
b	r	c	fl	sl

Nonsense Word Reading

flug	grib	flam	frin	blod
glub	wid	dem	heg	bap
vix	ed	glup	plob	wen
flob	trin	plid	swen	frix
jeld	vind	simp	gox	lub

Real Word Reading

Bob	sad	plan	jam	glad
yelp	blip	flax	beg	get
pal	yet	pin	met	box
lid	grab	plod	help	belt
vest	nut	tux	red	slop

Decoding Story 1.2: "Flip and Flop"

Section 2

Non-phonetic Word Recognition

Only read the real words in these paragraphs.

Wix fen the gliv frens glap too fip.
One grix brap two vens ix frep are int.
Flen grib from the jend fisp.
Cran frim have yub tilp wext.
Silb what dran give plit.

Swip yub the grix pid too fip.
One yub prab two lems id porf are ont.
Gren julb from the pisk felp.
Grom trux have nuv pilt twend.
Bild what groz give plax.

Yuv pex the drig frib ploz too gov.
One lif yorp two ud ont trib are und.
Plen brax from the yelb twixt.
Pilt grav have yoj kilf rund.
Sav what prax give selt.

Mox the too wext trest what give.
One frop liolpo have from dewn fisppp
Plen brax from the yelb twixt.
Hu hup yoildf one the int hytrf fcolvk
Ru clof have njghuy fspoil are what

Simps ott cdriu too the yuipol
Glup ed xim from the goiyt ug
Lub niou two adkje gtiop one ir
Fitly drkiuyt too one fut iw
Grin ute rtiut was the Rio lpoi

 Clark, J & McIntosh, M. (2022) *Just Read* © Pavilion Publishing and Media Ltd 2022.

Decoding Story 1.2: "Flip and Flop"

Section 3

Sentence Stacks

Flip and Flop

Flip and Flop were pals

Flip and Flop were pals from a

Flip and Flop were pals from a grand land.

Flip was glad

Flip was glad but

Flip was glad but Flop was

Flip was glad but Flop was sad.

Flop was

Flop was glad

Flop was glad to have

Flop was glad to have a lot of dogs.

Flip got

Flip got his pal Flop

Flip got his pal Flop to hop

Flip got his pal Flop to hop up and run.

Flip got

Flip got his pal Flop

Flip got his pal Flop to hop

Flip got his pal Flop to hop up and run.

Decoding Story 1.2: "Flip and Flop"

Section 4

Flip and Flop are pals from a grand land. In the land, Flip has a lot of dogs. Flip was a lad who put his dogs at the top. Flop had one dog. Flip was glad but Flop was sad as Flip did not have a lot of dogs. Flip went to get Flop to run with his dogs but Flop was too sad to run. Flip did give his pal Flop two dogs. Flip got his pal Flop to hop up and run. Flop was not sad. Flop was glad to have a lot of dogs. Flop got up to run with Flip and his dogs. What fun Flip and Flop had as they ran from spot to spot. Flop had the best dogs in the land. Flip and Flop are pals who are glad.

 Clark, J & McIntosh, M. (2022) *Just Read* © Pavilion Publishing and Media Ltd 2022.

Decoding Story 1.3: "Jan's Quilt"

Section 1

Isolated Phonogram Reading

gr	qu	fl	sp	cr
bl	st	f	mp	u
pl	sn	dr	qu	nd
lt	ft	st	r	e
nt	pt	tr	pl	fl

Nonsense Word Reading

quab	grox	lemp	fust	brasp
bint	snup	fruz	wemp	lund
lopt	brist	telp	treft	kisp
cruft	hund	squift	plox	reft
muxt	jept	grap	quelp	bisk

Real Word Reading

quilt	dog	mud	grab	jump
sad	red	pal	fast	lamp
grub	past	craft	graft	last
tub	bag	crab	dump	just
quit	flip	squid	lug	had

Decoding Story 1.3: "Jan's Quilt"

Section 2

Non-phonetic Word Recognition

Only read the real words in these paragraphs.

Trix wen have frin ip jost. Jelp was
un gat ep the glist.
Mesp brix gren to plid.
Twisp are drig was em frid.

Ftiyu piox clkiop was are whi uyt
iap Trough trie st to are the fgty
ot Fust tyue frist to are the lakrei
fi Kijhg typo have blopid are the yu

Drolp fiouist fip to the was
Saqwse fil ghto have the
to Wlklri frot the have bijgke ty
treft ghuj xewsd have polk pooit

Quelp the roiuty to the redfs
Thirfy to nmcnvb the serety
Ghvbcet to the have dfgopit ij
Dredsc ti seq wolpi are to glij

gholoiu have swa the to rfklj
fro jumolk to the roliuyj have muyte ut
klop the to yutyip gilet bvxesd foq
the nvboplit was the to have qoejkn

Decoding Story 1.3: "Jan's Quilt"

Section 3

Sentence Stacks

Sid had

Sid had the quilt

Sid had the quilt and did jump on it.

Sid ran to grab

Sid ran to grab Jan but Sid did not

Sid ran to grab Jan but Sid did not run fast.

Sid did

Sid did jump and jump

Sid did jump and jump and Jan was fed up.

Jan did grab

Jan did grab the quilt

Jan did grab the quilt and ran.

The quilt

The quilt had mud

The quilt had mud and Jan

The quilt had mud and Jan did not have

The quilt had mud and Jan did not have a pal in Sid.

Decoding Story 1.3: "Jan's Quilt"

Section 4

Jan had a quilt. This quilt was the best. It had a red dog on it.
Jan's mom did craft the quilt for Jan. Jan did grab the quilt to sit
on. Jan's pal Sid did grab the quilt. Jan was sad. Sid had the quilt
and did jump on it. The red dog on the quilt had mud on it. Jan was
mad. Sid did jump and jump and Jan was fed up. Jan did grab the
quilt and ran. Sid ran to grab Jan but Sid did not run fast. Sid did not
grab Jan. Jan quit the run. Sid and Jan are not pals. The quilt
had mud and Jan did not have a pal in Sid. Sid and Jan felt sad.

Story FP-1.1: "The Quiz"

Section 1

Isolated Phonogram Reading

qu	cl	pl	cr	gr
ck	qu	fr	br	sm
pl	gl	ck	tr	sw
bl	qu	fr	cr	dr
pr	tw	sk	ft	mp

Nonsense Word Reading

quet	vuck	bromp	quop	crund
splock	strind	flaz	brift	plon
quix	vick	quend	creft	sprip
wend	twib	juck	vind	quelp
cleck	strift	prump	jelp	drick

Real Word Reading

struck	clamp	quell	brick	back
plan	loft	quest	deck	clock
quiz	grand	grab	cram	jump
plot	stop	black	muck	quid
split	struck	lost	strip	quack

Story FP-1.1: "The Quiz"

Section 2

Non-phonetic Word Recognition

Only read the real words in these paragraphs.

crund flox tremp was grix
jund frimp have pord grusk lopt
trind fip give tru plemp to dilp
delp wux done wift fop hund

quia frimp to jud forg
swind brep milp have frut
trelp fid give turp to barx
wex frig tump brig was belp

Was rituyr tpolout done was to the ip
Dipole you qasdt foiuty was plaiasw you
Cilklmn dipole you from to the was you
Giuit ghytuo of the to from you have ew

Barxz cgfhyt was done tyeieh ewer driploiu
Vyterd from the to you djro iejou shof jrj to
Voojuty flooiuyt kwade qwiao gvie ytu powes
Molkji ahjoiy have grwaqst giuyt yuryt erst fro

rweyurt to the give noplert to the
have the give to the roisutp mollie your
myofia uint was the roiuty the hvae huy
qwsder folopi done the was to req to nedt

 Clark, J & McIntosh, M. (2022) *Just Read* © Pavilion Publishing and Media Ltd 2022.

Story FP-1.1: "The Quiz"

Section 3

Sentence Stacks

Quin was quick

Quin was quick to grab

Quin was quick to grab his pen

Quin was quick to grab his pen and run

Quin was quick to grab his pen and run up to his loft

Quin was quick to grab his pen and run up to his loft to print a map

Quin was quick to grab his pen and run up to his loft to print a map of his plan.

Quin's plan

Quin's plan was to

Quin's plan was to jam his plan

Quin's plan was to jam his plan in his bag

Quin's plan was to jam his plan in his bag and give it

Quin's plan was to jam his plan in his bag and give it to his pal Dan.

Quin had

Quin had a plan

Quin had a plan to cram

Quin had a plan to cram for the quiz.

Quin felt

Quin felt the quiz

Quin felt the quiz was

Quin felt the quiz was in the bag.

Quin did

Quin did not get

Quin did not get to the top

Quin did not get to the top of his class.

Story FP-1.1: "The Quiz"

Section 4

Quin was a guy who was on a quest. Quin's quest was to get to the top of his class. Quin had a plan to cram for the quiz. Quin was quick to grab his pen and run up to his loft to print a map of his plan. On his desk sat a big clock. The clock was from a pal. Quin's plan was to jam his plan in his bag and give it to his pal Dan. Quin had to map his big plan at the back of his loft. Quin was quick to map the plan. The plan was done. Quin felt the quiz was in the bag. Quin got to his class and met Dan. Dan did pat Quin on the back. The quiz was not on the plan. Mrs Jun had to pass on the plan to have a quiz. Quin did not get to the top of his class. Bad luck Quin.

Story FP-2.1: "The Lost Quilt"

Section 1

Isolated Phonogram Reading

qu	spl	str	mp	dr
a	ck	c	pl	k
e	sp	st	u	squ
l	ft	nd	nt	gl
scr	tw	st	sk	sw

Nonsense Word Reading

squip	fack	plom	med	plust
quif	yod	climp	nug	glon
spom	swif	flomp	frist	clof
flist	crill	Vost	quot	blist
drog	pron	Plant	snoft	lop

Real Word Reading

quest	squid	nob	bluff	floss
frog	track	dock	stump	pond
spot	tell	skip	glad	quilt
fast	trump	mess	squint	pick
rocks	black	twig	last	muck

Story FP-2.1: "The Lost Quilt"

Section 2

Non-phonetic Word Recognition

Only read the real words in these paragraphs.

Kipet unplo many narth plet
Only vab axd some fups hox
Come trub flin to speg
Skol some dexho tef pauy oj

Many raztim nolf kunch some
Ofent pog only uhert many
Only feag ykip how come
Tepit arjphat many fab veb

Some of the many to you was frif drgtop
Fjkhsjykt guidjfj many to the was frjhiuth
Jshtohrouh only Tod sjeh josijrij jhueh to
to ksjktj kzk thr skljt ir olmo done to the

Thujijar of the to you njfhth eu tref ploi
Diejr sht the some ahdf to the was you
The furhf jirh gyup do to the fro jhskjh
Fhiur to the was only jhsuht tfsj of

deaswqer only some rihsjdh come to you
was the kftuior to jskjytrj only frhtkh su tajs
the come some jdhtuhkjhjy jihfjskhur irwks
saberte ksjfrun kjshjkh come jiuhekj some

 Clark, J & McIntosh, M. (2022) *Just Read* © Pavilion Publishing and Media Ltd 2022.

Story FP-2.1: "The Lost Quilt"

Section 3

Sentence Stacks

They were so mad

They were so mad at the muck but

They were so mad at the muck but Quin got a twig

They were so mad at the muck but Quin got a twig and did pick it off.

Quin fled

Quin fled up the big hill

Quin fled up the big hill as fast as Quin did run

Quin fled up the big hill as fast as Quin did run and did belt a big yell.

Bess was

Bess was on a quest

Bess was on a quest to pick

Bess was on a quest to pick a black fleck rock

Bess was on a quest to pick a black fleck rock but Tess felt mad

Bess was on a quest to pick a black fleck rock but Tess felt mad and did a big yell.

Bess and Tess

Bess and Tess did squint

Bess and Tess did squint at him

Bess and Tess did squint at him and they ran back

Bess and Tess did squint at him and they ran back to the pond.

As luck did come,

As luck did come, Bess did put

As luck did come, Bess did put the quilt

As luck did come, Bess did put the quilt in a big clump

As luck did come, Bess did put the quilt in a big clump of black muck!

Story FP-2.1: "The Lost Quilt"

Section 4

Bess, Tess and Quin sat on the red quilt in the sun. They felt very cold and were to pick up many rocks for the pond in the back. Bess was on a quest for a black fleck rock but Tess felt mad and did a big yell. Quin felt they were too quick to pick up rocks and did skip back to the quilt, but it was lost! Quick, Quin fled up the big hill as fast as the wind and he did belt a big yell "The red quilt is lost!!" Bess and Tess did squint at him and they ran back to the pond. As luck did come, Bess did put the quilt in a big clump of black muck! It was a big mess! Who put the quilt in the muck? Bess did drop and roll it in the grass to get the muck off, but it was stuck! They were so mad at the muck but Quin got a twig and did pick it off. They were back on the red quilt and felt the sun at last.

    Clark, J & McIntosh, M. (2022) *Just Read* © Pavilion Publishing and Media Ltd 2022.

Story FP-3.1: "Seth's Trip on a Ship"

Section 1

Isolated Phonogram Reading

th	sh	tr	ch	gr
bl	nd	ch	lt	mp
nt	th	pl	tw	shr
thr	bl	gr	fl	st
pt	sh	pt	sw	fr

Nonsense Word Reading

chud	thrip	flum	shub	trux
shrag	jund	prib	twuv	wolp
flej	venft	swib	thiz	vind
sprox	brub	glopt	thag	prilk
wemp	prax	glud	dimp	rext

Real Word Reading

lunch	grab	with	rush	jump
that	help	told	gal	ship
did	stop	man	back	bump
bench	stub	flop	branch	fix
bath	kelp	dump	lock	welt

Story FP-3.1: "Seth's Trip on a Ship"

Section 2

Non-phonetic Word Recognition

Only read the real words in these paragraphs.

sprif grib many twix crub
groft premp trif only druj klib
sprox frend truj pluv come
swiv trib frox many brins

frib veng drex croz come trij
wex criv blon only frim
reb brid frup some twibs
spleft wanch wuld many

f Many to come ahjthi u to the freh
Fitly osjg gtup one many some have
Fieshhj jail only some shukrkn the to
Janjkf cfut ajnjf j was to the you of

Jgnoshh to many jetjshd jej kje kj
Hjfkshekrh to shish kjhs you jshiuteh
Kjehkjh too usyrjn jhherukh are roi
jshgurhjn ksnlkeh ksjrie to the jhkjh many some

kjshktuh to done to have teuhrkjf hkjshj you ksjh
hrhuhone have to the jaheiuhru htiu skwull you
shituh done to sjkhtuehj k kjahk you noutnj jolrj
bjhsuhr was are rhtkuhut to hsiue bihroiuh obj to

Story FP-3.1: "Seth's Trip on a Ship"

Section 3

Sentence Stacks

Seth and Chad

Seth and Chad sat

Seth and Chad sat on the bench

Seth and Chad sat on the bench to have their lunch.

Seth told Chad

Seth told Chad that some guys

Seth told Chad that some guys were on the ship

Seth told Chad that some guys were on the ship and they did help Seth.

The man

The man did wish

The man did wish to have a swim

The man did wish to have a swim but went back

The man did wish to have a swim but went back to his flat

The man did wish to have a swim but went back to his flat on the ship.

Seth and the gal

Seth and the gal did pat

Seth and the gal did pat the man's back

Seth and the gal did pat the man's back and were glad

Seth and the gal did pat the man's back and were glad that the man

Seth and the gal did pat the man's back and were glad that the man did not jump ship.

The man

The man did wish

The man did wish to have a swim

The man did wish to have a swim but went back

The man did wish to have a swim but went back to his flat

Chad was glad that Seth and the gal did help the man.

Story FP-3.1: "Seth's Trip on a Ship"

Section 4

Seth met Chad for lunch. Seth was in a rush to tell Chad of his clash with a man on a ship. Seth and Chad sat on the bench to have their lunch. Seth said, "The man on the ship was in a rush to jump ship to go for a swim!" Seth said that a gal had to stop the man. Seth and the gal did grab the man. The gal did yell to the man, "Come back!" as she did pull the man back from the end of the ship. Seth told Chad that some guys were on the ship and they did help Seth and the gal with the man. Seth and the gal did pat the man's back and were glad that the man did not jump ship. The man did wish to have a swim but went back to his flat on the ship. Seth told Chad that he was glad that the man did not jump ship. Chad was glad that Seth and the gal did help the man.

Story FP-3.1: "Seth's Trip on a Ship"

 Clark, J & McIntosh, M. (2022) *Just Read* © Pavilion Publishing and Media Ltd 2022.

Story FP-4.1: "At the Pond"

Section 1

Isolated Phonogram Reading

th	sh	qu	u	e
tch	dge	nd	st	ch
wh	ing	ank	mp	str
tch	fl	scr	ft	xt
ck	thr	shr	spl	dge

Nonsense Word Reading

lomp	grimp	flind	drunch	flodge
widge	brudge	clonch	blest	swutch
flink	druck	dradge	slish	crench
shump	drump	wensh	scomp	skitch
swong	blomp	dreck	wemp	plish

Real Word Reading

flesh	trudge	fridge	switch	hedge
hand	notch	french	drench	with
ledge	shrimp	clutch	belch	crash
chest	frill	less	stretch	squint
bath	blush	squish	bench	thick

Story FP-4.1: "At the Pond"

Section 2

Non-phonetic Word Recognition

Only read the real words in these paragraphs.

Hals yed sida sure jik pos only
Quext door both nom diff guy
Floor def gex iuhump gblop once
Jiopl floj both only dape cvol

Both thiurhut sure the was jshtu acvsh the
Hfjkhksuhj hedfkr typeer sure only to
Njdhsuh both floor sjkeuhrj too shuej
Djsurh once sjhrieuhrj once kjshj to

Only once kjshkjfhdkjhf to jkskdjh
From the floor to the door anjr to
Sjhdkjh xwes you are shthsjh vgtuy
Jkjshkfkjs to the door sure on the

Oahu floor t the hjhkjh khaki was done iutyo
hfure do you what the are was ouhebjh btui
you are jskduh floor you sjkkuhd krjhgj kjfg
skjkjh floor was kjshrkush have what jusdk

you have skjhtkjhskh the ksjhfkjhs pol jfue
sjkhkjhkth kjhthehj to the you was only sjhtu
ksjh kjrht once jhskhfsh what jshh to
many flurg have ponb only yulg what to

Story FP-4.1: "At the Pond"

Section 3

Sentence Stacks

Chad had to ask

Chad had to ask if it was ok

Chad had to ask if it was ok and his

Chad had to ask if it was ok and his dad said yes.

Once they were

Once they were at the pond

Once they were at the pond Chad did spot

Once they were at the pond Chad did spot his friend Hodge

But just then

But just then Tuck did

But just then Tuck did a fast spin

But just then Tuck did a fast spin and did snatch

But just then Tuck did a fast spin and did snatch a very big patch

But just then Tuck did a fast spin and did snatch a very big patch of twigs from the grass.

As they ran

As they ran on the path,

As they ran on the path, they both did smell

As they ran on the path, they both did smell a lush

As they ran on the path, they both did smell a lush and splendid smell.

With a stick

With a stick in hand,

With a stick in hand, Chad bent

With a stick in hand, Chad bent to the path

With a stick in hand, Chad bent to the path and hid

With a stick in hand, Chad bent to the path and hid in the long,

With a stick in hand, Chad bent to the path and hid in the long, tall grass.

Story FP-4.1: "At the Pond"

Section 4

Once, Chad and his dog Tuck went to visit his pal at the pond. Chad had to ask if it was ok and his dad said yes. Chad and Tuck did a quick dash and cut past the kitchen on the path to the back door. They did a big jump off the back deck and did land in the tall, wet grass. They were sure that they were ok and kept on the run. As they ran on the path, they both did smell a lush and splendid smell. The plants were big, soft and plush and some were red and some were just a bud. Along the top of the tall hedge, Chad and Tuck did a quick scan for trash but did not get any. Once they were at the pond, Chad did spot his pal Hodge. Hodge said that the frogs and fish were on the logs and snacking on lunch but if they were still, they could watch. With a stick in hand, Chad bent to the path and hid in the long, tall grass. But just then, Tuck did a fast spin and did snatch a very big patch of twigs from the grass. He did sniff and smell but did not yelp. The frogs and fish were quick to dash and hid in the sand and logs. Too bad! Tuck ran off and Chad and Hodge had to miss the fish. They were mad!

Story FP-5.1: "Stash the Cash"

Section 1

Isolated Phonogram Reading

sh	ch	nt	dge	ong
th	spl	nd	ank	ink
str	mp	pr	spl	old
qu	sk	ft	bl	shr
ck	str	thr	fl	ang

Nonsense Word Reading

dold	mank	prunk	fless	squast
rist	plis	flonk	shrick	jib
ront	splosh	glud	shrift	losh
blift	prunt	lench	trop	bluss
flust	hod	dist	blesk	plis

Real Word Reading

all	had	quick	stash	judge
went	back	next	trudge	bench
rent	cash	check	best	long
print	spent	insist	blank	lodge
switch	blank	lodge	desk	sprint

Story FP-5.1: "Stash the Cash"

Section 2

Non-phonetic Word Recognition

Only read the real words in these paragraphs.

Grist mot very trop much here har mest
flink Here holp very such dest clom plosh cit drow
climp vist here olp vump blom clop glip

Frim bul glid move both yut trop jesk huy
nodge frit op glod move plok move
Don't yih jut rund flor four nil buh

One very sskuh ghjrh jdjhr here much
Don't hsihreuh one of jskjheuh sjhekjh
The kjhskjhjh both here very to the you
The kjhskjhjh both here very to the you

skjhkjth jsrtjn knto the door shh h both
sjkjthjh hsjkh kj the to you jsnkjhjh lpj
was jshektjh ifgh kojhf jshr kjsu both
move to grib such one pind the yurb porb

move to here attunjf you jhrb jb do the
very lskjitu you jsntku Jon ifhgt skhjt po
here Kolp much onhty jshruh much anrf
Don't both ksekjhr the kskjher some

 Clark, J & McIntosh, M. (2022) *Just Read* © Pavilion Publishing and Media Ltd 2022.

Story FP-5.1: "Stash the Cash"

Section 3

Sentence Stacks

When King Frank

When King Frank wished for cash,

When King Frank wished for cash, he went

When King Frank wished for cash, he went to his press

When King Frank wished for cash, he went to his press that could

When King Frank wished for cash, he went to his press that could print cash.

Frank wished

Frank wished for cash

Frank wished for cash that would

Frank wished for cash that would help his fans.

Frank's plan

Frank's plan was to stash

Frank's plan was to stash the cash

Frank's plan was to stash the cash so that his pals

Frank's plan was to stash the cash so that his pals could not

Frank's plan was to stash the cash so that his pals could not grab it.

When the clock

When the clock struck two,

When the clock struck two, King Frank hitched

When the clock struck two, King Frank hitched a lock

When the clock struck two, King Frank hitched a lock on the press

When the clock struck two, King Frank hitched a lock on the press and packed it in his trunk.

It was then

It was then that King Frank's pals

It was then that King Frank's pals could not

It was then that King Frank's pals could not grab the cash.

Story FP-5.1: "Stash the Cash"

Section 4

Frank was a king who spent a lot of cash. When King Frank wished for cash, he went to his press that could print cash. Frank stashed his cash in a trunk at the back of his desk. Frank would run to his press a lot to print cash. A bunch of Frank's pals would take his cash and run to clubs to spend and spend his cash. Frank did not want his pals to snatch his cash and he did not want to run to the clubs with his pals. Frank wished for cash that would help his fans. With a dash, Frank ran to his press that had the last batch of cash on it. When the clock struck two, King Frank hitched a lock on the press and packed it in his trunk. Quick as a flash, King Frank dashed up the hill to the edge of the kingdom clutching the trunk with the last bunch of cash that was hot off the press. Frank's plan was to stash the cash so that his pals could not grab it. Frank did stash the cash at the back of the shed with the help of his friend, Mitch. It was then that King Frank's pals could not grab the cash. King Frank ended up with a lot of cash that he was glad he could spend and stash.

Clark, J & McIntosh, M. (2022) *Just Read* © Pavilion Publishing and Media Ltd 2022.

Story FP 6.1: "The Back Lane"

Section 1

Isolated Phonogram Reading

tch	a-e	e-e	ing	unk
dge	i-e	sh	o-e	ink
ung	ank	ung	mp	squ
eng	thr	ong	ank	a-e
qu	onk	ing	o-e	ink

Nonsense Word Reading

jidge	smotch	drong	plong	swutch
vank	thronk	clong	plang	dridge
slove	clave	plide	brose	kank
flong	trife	smole	smate	loke
snode	swoft	pleft	nime	blude

Real Word Reading

smile	rode	black	truck	joke
slide	crutch	glitch	bike	drape
chive	made	shed	drive	hope
blade	drench	bad	like	kick
vote	sell	flute	trade	brave

Story FP 6.1: "The Back Lane"

Section 2

Non-phonetic Word Recognition

Only read the real words in these paragraphs.

Lin boach nerf molk mother orlop
Solp raph which heif sufght
Dpol mims ful another those
Frile queth olp irpla brother

Abic mond hinr other which
Another blimp drox mib
Aqws dunt monter uytheor
Which greem dus lofha other

Brother jhkdur jnuern only was the ti
Other to the jndkjfhujnak jeer lkjr ssoej
Kjshthj which only to the both snkjh jekjs
Rjhtkjhkh only some Coe kjrntjks some

Djshuihj noi jksnkuht the to many to
Both kodjrd to the some artkrt other
Another which sjhtiu hj clifg are too je
Hgjkerh drjhe ndkjh monther sure

eajke another tekj jksjh was the skjgkse
ksjkjth jnsjtkjhakjh jshekj ekjfuhksj to you
both another shoufg mother ajngskj to re
come to the jsekjht another jnsjhdg which

 Clark, J & McIntosh, M. (2022) *Just Read* © Pavilion Publishing and Media Ltd 2022.

Story FP 6.1: "The Back Lane"

Section 3

Sentence Stacks

All of them
All of them had the same
All of them had the same black truck
All of them had the same black truck as they liked
All of them had the same black truck as they liked the shape and the shade

The man
The man who gave
The man who gave Mike the cash
The man who gave Mike the cash said that
The man who gave Mike the cash said that he would sell the bike
The man who gave Mike the cash said that he would sell the bike back to Steve

As he drove,
As he drove, Mike sang
As he drove, Mike sang a long sad song
As he drove, Mike sang a long sad song that made him
As he drove, Mike sang a long sad song that made him smile with pride.

When the
When the date came,
When the date came, they made
When the date came, they made a big mistake
When the date came, they made a big mistake and sold
When the date came, they made a big mistake and sold Steve's bike.

Steve was
Steve was still mad
Steve was still mad but did invite
Steve was still mad but did invite the man
Steve was still mad but did invite the man to take
Steve was still mad but did invite the man to take a quick spin
Steve was still mad but did invite the man to take a quick spin up the lane.

Story FP 6.1: "The Back Lane"

Section 4

Mike is a man who likes to drive too fast all of the time. One day, when it was late, Mike went to the back shed and put all of his junk in the back of his black truck and sped off. As he drove, Mike sang a long sad song that made him smile with pride. As he went to finish his drive, on the side of the back lane, Mike met his friend Clive and they had a very long chat. They had no time to waste and told jokes and then bumped into an old bud Steve. All of them had the same black truck as they liked the shape and the shade. When they finished telling jokes, they made a plan to have a theme sale to get rid of some of the junk and stuff that was kept in the shack at the side of Mike's home. When the date came, they made a big mistake and sold Steve's bike. He was upset and mad because it was his red and white bike and it had bells and brakes that could help him stop. The man who gave Mike the cash said that he would sell the bike back to Steve if he could have a quick ride. Steve was still mad but did invite the man to take a quick spin up the lane. In the end, it was fine and all of them went to Mike's and made a funny joke.

Story FP 6.1: "The Back Lane"

Story FP-7.1: "Mad Ants"

Section 1

Isolated Phonogram Reading

a-e	ang	shr	dge	s-e
bl	s-e	nd	tch	all
all	ink	pt	mp	thr
e-e	unk	onk	xt	J
ing	dr	tr	spl	cl

Nonsense Word Reading

grall	kose	splive	scrope	Vall
dromp	flump	trimp	swape	dong
slitch	smame	flotch	ming	swunk
fose	drole	snodge	clonk	frint
rall	stope	clidge	drong	frest

Real Word Reading

nose	pal	grass	yell
grump	stung	mope	up
stung	wall	rose	bike
tall	fall	small	slope
hill	scrape	drive	brave

Story FP-7.1: "Mad Ants"

Section 2

Non-phonetic Word Recognition

Only read the real words in these paragraphs.

Pokoh bulz kloph again neel
Citad raph gule would could dunt
Ghyup every lyp jibt often phun
Nerf where again jave mize often

Corab again often thox thip
pight ref travin could kear smaser
Lif again periz bezy helf miel salm
Rap where should thonx neyert tro

Every often could jnkwhk jetful kjh to ou
Where again ti h&j often kjhr lj should ti
Jkshdiuh again where here skjtj nsjh tre
Kjhuh often sjeui could jshetu from the

Jksdanrn some ti njeh jahrj tho to
Sjhb some very would josh ouy re
Again the from very to do you to the
Ksjn unseen jkanother bjhsehui some

skjuh which where shthskj again ti kjhek to
could fjhsuh from the sjhiuh very
ksjkjh ty ksjndkth yught sr scola jajht again thunk
jskuht should ksjhkuht would jusgt come

Story FP-7.1: "Mad Ants"

Section 3

Sentence Stacks

While the dogs

While the dogs were running,

While the dogs were running, Pal got stung

While the dogs were running, Pal got stung on the nose

While the dogs were running, Pal got stung on the nose by a very big ant.

When they looked

When they looked at the hill,

When they looked at the hill, a line of red ants

When they looked at the hill, a line of red ants had sprung up

When they looked at the hill, a line of red ants had sprung up next to Steve's dog.

Jed was standing

Jed was standing next to the hill

Jed was standing next to the hill and dug a hole

Jed was standing next to the hill and dug a hole on the ant hill.

Off he ran,

Off he ran, into the long

Off he ran, into the long blades of crab

Off he ran, into the long blades of crab grass to hide.

Steve and Mike

Steve and Mike ran into

Steve and Mike ran into the grass

Steve and Mike ran into the grass to help Pal.

Story FP-7.1: "Mad Ants"

Section 4

Mike and his dog Jed like to run and sprint up hills. One time when they ran, they met Steve who also liked to run with his dog Pal. They both liked to trick the dogs and run and hide when the dogs chased the ball. While the dogs ran, Pal got stung on the nose by a very big ant. It was red and mad that Pal was standing on his ant-hill home. Pal ran back to Steve and all of them went to the hill. Jed was standing next to the hill and dug a hole on the ant hill. Mike spoke up and told Jed to stop with the dig. Jed had to stop. When they looked at the hill, a line of red ants had sprung up next to Steve's dog, but Pal did not think. Off he ran, into the long blades of crab grass to hide. The ants stopped to think and then gave up. Steve and Mike ran into the grass to help Pal. Jed ran too. At the end of the run, they all came back home and ate a snack. It was a long, hot time, but they had not got stung.

 Clark, J & McIntosh, M. (2022) *Just Read* © Pavilion Publishing and Media Ltd 2022.

Story FP-8.1: "Class Tricks"

Section 1

Isolated Phonogram Reading

y	e	a-e	all	a-e
o-e	th	i-e	str	u-e
tr	ing	ang	qu	e-e
mp	lt	str	spl	dge
ong	dr	ch	tch	ank

Nonsense Word Reading

py	scome	bolob	co	Fete
smi	drave	mi	lospil	ty
Fo	swaxe	pise	cly	clatch
Pa	lave	sny	slogum	drall
plerut	satrim	clomy	flave	mu

Real Word Reading

strapping	try	pretend	rotund	remit
swimming	dry	go	she	brink
slave	prefab	comply	going	fry
nose	grabbing	sting	brave	hose
spry	tide	present	ruse	rose

Story FP-8.1: "Class Tricks"

Section 2

Non-phonetic Word Recognition

Only read the real words in these paragraphs.

Turh yelasd could nolf lugah often nesund sreef
Should again sarl tiusnull facklo thuwd sluj dow
Gyurt you dat there got bhim quap molki here hawp
Arg again for slib gamd klup lepton

Raus often thuw perl tepid pacy would
Nait Penh ku again should qwas vblop
Pafrif mon cher pal here duig rok
There bs kola himz quiz dint often

Here tr hotefg jdifjiej again too the
Here tr hotefg jdifjiej again too the
Flair goupr sijoji some come to plods
Tjsiu both come sjoejt skijor dkjstioj

Jkhsuid skjrei olksjn oh one to js
Would you ftry skjher kksjerh fyi
Skjheru again eh hah jhwould too
Sjhrtuh would should jkshrkt kjdsut

hejrk gooijht the often where some too
hifdjstjn Gorki hahu ofetn could vblop
there are you some come skjfie tihskj
dkjiy where here ksjeioj from the sj very

 Clark, J & McIntosh, M. (2022) *Just Read* © Pavilion Publishing and Media Ltd 2022.

Story FP-8.1: "Class Tricks"

Section 3

Sentence Stacks

Dan began to justify

Dan began to justify why they all broke

Dan began to justify why they all broke but Trish began to cry

Dan began to justify why they all broke but Trish began to cry with a frustrated sob.

Just then

Just then Trish and Beth

Just then Trish and Beth rode by on their bikes

Just then Trish and Beth rode by on their bikes and asked them

Just then Trish and Beth rode by on their bikes and asked them what they were up to.

They asked

They asked if they could help

They asked if they could help with the planning

They asked if they could help with the planning as they were quick

They asked if they could help with the planning as they were quick and would like to win

They asked if they could help with the planning as they were quick and would like to win the prize.

Every time

Every time they filled

Every time they filled it too much,

Every time they filled it too much, the glove would explode

Every time they filled it too much, the glove would explode and drench

Every time they filled it too much, the glove would explode and drench them all.

He told them

He told them to put the glove

He told them to put the glove in the sun

He told them to put the glove in the sun so it would

He told them to put the glove in the sun so it would get hot

He told them to put the glove in the sun so it would get hot and it would expand.

Story FP-8.1: "Class Tricks"

Section 4

One day, Steve and Dan were busy trying to make a latex glove into a hand that could catch liquid. In class, Mr. Fry said whoever could do it would win a prize. Steve and Dan began to try many tricks but they began to regret the task because it was so difficult. Just then, Trish and Beth came over and asked them what they were up to. Both Beth and Trish were in Steve and Dan's class, so they coveted the prize too. Trish wanted to be the one to think of the best plan but Dan would not let her and demanded they all have equal input into the task. They began to fill many gloves up but all of them broke. Dan began to justify why they all broke and Trish began to cry with anger. Dan said they should modify one thing and they all nodded. Steve and Dan held the latex glove while Beth and Trish bent over them hugging the jug as they filled the glove. Every time they filled it too much, the glove would explode and drench them all. Just then, Steve had a winning bid. He told them to put the glove in the sun so it would get hot and it would expand. Again, Steve and Dan held the glove while Trish and Beth held onto the big jug. It worked! The gloves were full. Trish yelled and hopped on one leg as she sang out a tune.

 Clark, J & McIntosh, M. (2022) *Just Read* © Pavilion Publishing and Media Ltd 2022.

Story FP 9.1: "Jay's Fishing Trip"

Section 1

Isolated Phonogram Reading

ai	ea	qu	ay	ee
aw	tch	dge	ch	ea
th	ang	unk	ing	ct
ch	aw	ai	ea	ay
ea	spr	ee	sh	th

Nonsense Word Reading

bish	fleep	scraim	hawn	prodge
felch	creat	blay	stry	bu
treap	pawg	gream	teeping	trotch
kidge	shelped	thay	gry	pilped
tremmed	relfed	tring	glink	twifted

Real Word Reading

fishing	grabbed	unpacked	snagged
shrimp	happy	hoping	edge
drawback	baited	casted	waited
mistaken	agreed	sadly	switched
great	himself	fresh	stuff

Story FP 9.1: "Jay's Fishing Trip"

Section 2

Non-phonetic Word Recognition

Only read the real words in these paragraphs.

Scrimp flug triv welb would fimp
Glead freg shrop people exip twog
Trav splob tren frig answer wunch frib
prong crub vid want ud crax trill

Preeg felp trid frin glot father
Slirp gorb cpux the answer rint
Swuv torp would julp meng
Lorpoot ferb people wip tremp

Faikjse soho father one should jfhe
Jesjk too gigu sone want answer ty
Gjurshu froyou both people want yu
Flipe polkim rjsio kaj answer both from

Sjkj sikh cvt you do from was jhang
Jjh humh would ksjht want could oul
Skjh fussre answer people toojso iy
Portemp trem people piv freen

jdshiuuh hdcit kjdhf would people ksje
shah gorb huj answer wanr crux some
kjdkjh cvoif want both sure do the qieuiou
koi where the ikol milkf would nkjnsj bvfrt

Story FP 9.1: "Jay's Fishing Trip"

Section 3

Sentence Stacks

Jean grabbed
Jean grabbed all of their
Jean grabbed all of their fishing stuff
Jean grabbed all of their fishing stuff hoping to get
Jean grabbed all of their fishing stuff hoping to get on the trail
Jean grabbed all of their fishing stuff hoping to get on the trail by nine o'clock.

After waiting
After waiting for a long time,
After waiting for a long time, Jay looked at Jean
After waiting for a long time, Jay looked at Jean and switched his bait
After waiting for a long time, Jay looked at Jean and switched his bait back to shrimp.

Jay and Jean
Jay and Jean both saw
Jay and Jean both saw that the best
Jay and Jean both saw that the best fishing bait
Jay and Jean both saw that the best fishing bait for the lake
Jay and Jean both saw that the best fishing bait for the lake was shrimp.

Jean felt
Jean felt that it was
Jean felt that it was a drawback
Jean felt that it was a drawback to bait his line
Jean felt that it was a drawback to bait his line with shrimp
Jean felt that it was a drawback to bait his line with shrimp so she gave
Jean felt that it was a drawback to bait his line with shrimp so she gave him a fly.

Jay looked
Jay looked at Jean
Jay looked at Jean and switched
Jay looked at Jean and switched his bait
Jay looked at Jean and switched his bait back to shrimp.

Story FP 9.1: "Jay's Fishing Trip"

Section 4

Jay and his friend Jean had a plan to go on a big fishing trip. The plan was to leave for their trip at dawn. Jean grabbed all of their fishing stuff hoping to get on the trail by nine o'clock. Jay rushed to put the bait in the pail. They set off on their trip. When they got to the lake, Jean unpacked their stuff and sat on the edge. Jay sat himself by the bay and baited his line with shrimp. Jean felt that it was a drawback to bait their lines with shrimp so she gave him a fly. Jean thought that the answer to catching fish would be baiting their lines with flies. Jay agreed and then baited his line with a fly. Jean said that he would be sure to catch a fish with a fly. Jay cast his line into the lake. He waited and waited but the fish did not bite. Jean was hoping that the fly would be the best bait but she was sadly mistaken. After waiting for a long time, Jay looked at Jean and switched his bait back to shrimp. Jay snagged a fish in a flash! For the rest of the day, Jay snagged many fish using shrimp as his bait. Jay and Jean both saw that the best fishing bait for the lake was shrimp. They went home with a pail full of fresh fish to eat.

 Clark, J & McIntosh, M. (2022) *Just Read* © Pavilion Publishing and Media Ltd 2022.

Story FP-10.1: "Herb the Hermit Crab"

Section 1

Isolated Phonogram Reading

ar	tch	er	dge	ing
sh	sm	ai	ee	or
ang	ay	ch	sw	cr
gl	br	ar	th	ee
or	sn	gl	ck	ong

Nonsense Word Reading

flarb	credge	glert	blorp	treeb
chorg	traip	blay	sweez	beax
twerb	creen	streck	fodge	vutch
swimp	prind	gorp	berx	frub
strock	parj	jimp	flind	twab

Real Word Reading

hermit	safe	kept	sadly
stretched	shell	claws	empty
stepped	picked	small	growing
looked	seemed	himself	fresh
edge	scratch	inside	squish

Story FP-10.1: "Herb the Hermit Crab"

Section 2

Non-phonetic Word Recognition

Only read the real words in these paragraphs.

fribum trop glorf rough himbot forb
twint fleg prat friend welb dring
strox flint minute junt med
splux crad enough helz trib

yud prob whix tough spilf grix
dep twind frob zelp dran during trid
swax fleep beav rough wend
torx feev raif minute jelp

Minute friend judos lskjt jiorjj could sord
Dis during where kjslkj lkjerk the folkx ij
Jeths jsirj some gjhjs ksjj nlskjelkj many
Hfkj jhkjehr ast koste enough soughtr to

Skjdjk swap jgskj minute kjdkj during
Splux the dkjrin friend ksisjirh tough
During lkddjok people skillk jslkje any
Jojnf kj nlknlkcrad kjlajrkej during jojh

jsrhituh firicg during should do pjs jkjsht
ksljdtldjk friend during was draftinh enough
many kshtl both skuhktjhkj jumgh khsuhe
kjsjh roughvb lkliehrlh friend during grjasujoj

 Clark, J & McIntosh, M. (2022) *Just Read* © Pavilion Publishing and Media Ltd 2022.

Story FP-10.1: "Herb the Hermit Crab"

Section 3

Sentence Stacks

When Herb's friends

When Herb's friends would ask him

When Herb's friends would ask him to come out and play,

When Herb's friends would ask him to come out and play, he never wanted to

When Herb's friends would ask him to come out and play, he never wanted to because he was afraid.

He stretched out

He stretched out his legs and claws

He stretched out his legs and claws and stepped out

He stretched out his legs and claws and stepped out from his shell.

Herb was glad

Herb was glad in his new home

Herb was glad in his new home and he was

Herb was glad in his new home and he was safe once again.

He tapped

He tapped on it

He tapped on it with his claws

He tapped on it with his claws and it was empty.

Herb now

Herb now had a fresh

Herb now had a fresh and flawless shell

Herb now had a fresh and flawless shell to keep him safe.

Story FP-10.1: "Herb the Hermit Crab"

Section 4

Herb was a hermit crab who was scared of everything. Herb was glad to have a shell to hide in. When Herb's friends would ask him to come out and play, he never wanted to because he was afraid. Herb's shell kept him safe. Herb had carefully picked this shell after his last shell got too small for his growing body.

One day, Herb woke up feeling very cramped. Herb's legs couldn't move like they used to and his claws were bunched up inside of his shell. Suddenly, Herb's body felt too big for his shell. His legs were squished inside and his claws scratched the edges of his shell. As Herb found it tough to move around in the shell that he loved, he now saw what he had to do. Herb had to find a new shell. Herb looked around his shell and sadly said goodbye. He stretched out his legs and claws and stepped out from his shell. Herb was very scared as he crawled along the sand with no shell. Soon, he came upon a shell that seemed to be the best fit. He tapped on it with his claws and it was empty. He made sure that no other crabs were using the shell and he was in luck. Herb moved himself into the new shell. Herb now had a fresh and flawless shell to keep him safe. Herb was glad in his new home and he was safe once again.

Story FP-11.1: "Anne Bonny"

Section 1

Isolated Phonogram Reading

oy	er	qu	i-e	a-e
ee	or	ay	dge	oo
oa	Ea	e-e	tch	ow
oo	aw	spl	ee	oi
ow	ar	nt	oa	ck

Nonsense Word Reading

toger	doof	slowd	coig	sloy
riholm	forgim	veet	slawt	cloam
swain	clouse	neem	hoom	corm
froil	doy	pook	vouse	swoil
Bloy	tarf	dreaf	garm	loag

Real Word Reading

secret	pirate	open	deploy
soak	spoon	toil	loot
disappoint	ploy	moist	unload
grown	oyster	rejoin	coins
sailed	quite	popular	relocate

Story FP-11.1: "Anne Bonny"

Section 2

Non-phonetic Word Recognition

Only read the real words in these paragraphs.

Yabel clop blood revery tac
Tique nare dow ghyu vfg
Sugar Peab hool Thaip
Whose truth laugh etach

Wohy cvolk laugh uyomh
Charght sugar feahp faber
Whose blood whoes bolood
Frimp twix whose yump crub

Sugar osh je jhksjh friend to the sjfng
Skjtjij dcf iuisjodj klsjljr father hrigo
should dkjiy the to ejsjhk jaj friend sef
Isoifoiej sehr hhhjhajrh jhkjahjrh jh to

Sljsekj jhsej huh jekhtkj hjkehtjh jhtt js
Laugh whose kjhtj hajkh jahehr jhakjeh
Sjhr jaj jalhrh ajar hahah ah would do the
Jkeht karhlk ka should could would tp kan

laugh jkhaerhuh whose blodd kjharuh skjerr
blood sugar the ws any bosouji jahrioh
kdjflkjadkfj kljreh kkjkue khrjakjh sugar who
sjhejrh njkahrejh whose blllud jwhejkh laugh

   Clark, J & McIntosh, M. (2022) *Just Read* © Pavilion Publishing and Media Ltd 2022.

Story FP-11.1: "Anne Bonny"

Section 3

Sentence Stacks

Her ship

Her ship was pounced on

Her ship was pounced on and raided

Her ship was pounced on and raided and all the pirates

Her ship was pounced on and raided and all the pirates were taken away

Her ship was pounced on and raided and all the pirates were taken away to the prison.

During the 1800s

During the 1800s when pirates

During the 1800s when pirates were the most popular

During the 1800s when pirates were the most popular, Anne left her easy life

During the 1800s when pirates were the most popular, Anne left her easy life for one of extreme adventure.

Anne Bonny

Anne Bonny should be remembered

Anne Bonny should be remembered as being a

Anne Bonny should be remembered as being a strong female

Anne Bonny should be remembered as being a strong female who refused to be

Anne Bonny should be remembered as being a strong female who refused to be a standard woman.

She tried to keep

She tried to keep her identity

She tried to keep her identity a secret

She tried to keep her identity a secret and often

She tried to keep her identity a secret and often dressed like a man.

She sailed

She sailed on private ships

She sailed on private ships in the open

She sailed on private ships in the open sea looting trading ships

She sailed on private ships in the open sea looting trading ships and stealing

She sailed on private ships in the open sea looting trading ships and stealing coins, gold and silver.

Story FP-11.1: "Anne Bonny"

Section 4

Have you ever heard the tale of the first female pirate? Well, she is quite popular. Her name is Anne Bonny. She was born in the 1700s in Ireland and then moved to the United States when she was a baby. Why was she so famous? She was the first female to be recognized as a pirate.

During the 1800s, when pirates were the most popular, Anne left her easy life for one of extreme adventure. She tried to keep her identity a secret and often dressed like a man. She sailed on private ships in the open sea looting trading ships and stealing coins, gold and silver. Her life was one of loyalty and fun while being a pirate. Her adventure finished one day when she was aboard the ship "William". Her ship was pounced on and raided and all the pirates were taken away to the prison. Anne Bonny's captain John Rackman was put to death but Anne, it was decided, should skip the hanging because she as a woman! Later, it was found out that Bonny's father had secured her release and she was relocated back to her home where she rejoined her father and later married and had four children of her own. Reports of her death are pegged in 1782. Anne Bonny should be remembered as being a strong female who refused to be a standard woman.

Story FP-12.1: "The RMS Titanic – A Canadian Connection"

Section 1

Isolated Phonogram Reading

ea	u-e	ing	g	c
ink	tch	tion	unk	th
all	i-e	y	old	ung
e-e	onk	o-e	ang	str
ee	th	ai	spl	ch

Nonsense Word Reading

nold	trang	bufe	strifting	brunded
plotion	franzic	swelping	grufted	preld
winted	grunding	twiftion	sprong	twing
libeful	hunded	dribness	juxted	splinded
huve	pri	lintop	frixveb	troxted

Real Word Reading

people	actually	tragedy	special
museum	ocean	unsinkable	concert
bodies	exhibit	occasion	iceberg
permanent	claimed	rescued	impacted
liner	dispatched	century	arrived

Story FP-12.1: "The RMS Titanic – A Canadian Connection"

Section 2

Non-phonetic Word Recognition

Only read the real words in these paragraphs.

Sprib flemp twing blood werf traig
Harb greap whose wen fitch splond
Mexib wrand fring laugh un twixted
Rebay sugar memp wratch blex

Rebaun youg graiv sugar punvid
Jextrip whose vendog helbing prox
Whifter rempid preng laugh twip
Skitch blood lextrop frind

Klsjt blood treijanf jeje jjhlhr laugh should you
Kjsdhhtj laugh hjkshj ketkjh whose klejlktj kej
Shtjh sdlhth lkerlk hslkhtlsflsdif laugh the to
Jskheth. Skhetlh kshjhakjhr jkayou to do the

Jshdjkhj hjshjk laugh fwho blood jhsa
To the was jehteo eojh hfjkahr akjhr kahru
Could blood jhesrh smh jh jhfla laugh krjt
Jsheth kjtk lskhklht hsleht lsh from teh

kjhth you nskjfhsfjkjhduieto do the was jras
kjt lkjslj kjblood whose sjhth lhtlkhetkhs lksjt
kdjhroit jrlktu would sejtsi who too
setlksje hsjjkshjsehtkj the should four both

Story FP-12.1: "The RMS Titanic –
A Canadian Connection"

Section 3

Sentence Stacks

It's hard to find

It's hard to find anyone that

It's hard to find anyone that does not know

It's hard to find anyone that does not know the story of

It's hard to find anyone that does not know the story of the Titanic.

To this day,

To this day, you can visit

To this day, you can visit the Maritime Museum

To this day, you can visit the Maritime Museum in Halifax

To this day, you can visit the Maritime Museum in Halifax which has a permanent

To this day, you can visit the Maritime Museum in Halifax which has a permanent Titanic exhibit.

Sadly,

Sadly, no survivors were found

Sadly, no survivors were found but several bodies

Sadly, no survivors were found but several bodies were found

Sadly, no survivors were found but several bodies were found and buried in

Sadly, no survivors were found but several bodies were found and buried in Halifax, Nova Scotia.

More than 1,500 people

More than 1,500 people were lost

More than 1,500 people were lost but more than

More than 1,500 people were lost but more than 700 people survived

More than 1,500 people were lost but more than 700 people survived and were rescued.

The RMS Titanic

The RMS Titanic was the largest

The RMS Titanic was the largest ocean liner

The RMS Titanic was the largest ocean liner of its time

The RMS Titanic was the largest ocean liner of its time and was claimed

The RMS Titanic was the largest ocean liner of its time and was claimed to be unsinkable.

Story FP-12.1: "The RMS Titanic – A Canadian Connection"

Section 4

It's hard to find anyone that does not know the story of the Titanic. The RMS Titanic was the largest ocean liner of its time and was claimed to be unsinkable. But, on April 14, 1912, the great ship struck an iceberg and sunk to the bottom of the ocean in only two hours and forty minutes. More than 1,500 people were lost but more than 700 people survived and were rescued. What most people don't know is that the day before the rescued passengers were to arrive in New York, the White Star Line had dispatched four Canadian ships to look for victims of the disaster. Sadly, no survivors were found but several bodies were found and buried in Halifax, Nova Scotia. What most people also do not know is that the RMS Titanic actually sunk in the North Atlantic water just off the coast of Halifax, Nova Scotia, in Canadian waters. The tragedy impacted the Canadian town so much that even today, after the liner hit the iceberg over a century ago, the city of Halifax still holds concerts, readings and special events to mark the occasion. To this day, you can visit the Maritime Museum in Halifax which has a permanent Titanic exhibit.

This story of international cooperation is a testament to how nations can work together in times of tragedy. It also reminds us that Canadians played a sad but important role in the aftermath of this awful disaster.

 Clark, J & McIntosh, M. (2022) *Just Read* © Pavilion Publishing and Media Ltd 2022.

Story FP-13.1: "The Origin of Castles"

Section 1

Isolated Phonogram Reading

fle	cle	gle	ew	ple
oo	or	er	ea	ph
ow	aw	ct	igh	oi
tle	nd	stle	oa	igh
zle	oy	ur	u-e	lr

Nonsense Word Reading

paple	cruddle	dect	trafle	shurgle
vight	braph	flaph	smoat	inkle
biddle	snazzle	slird	bloof	smay
snead	clow	phine	clouf	drail
wuffle	glight	frect	dritch	bact

Real Word Reading

cable	aspect	simple	rekindle
puzzle	compact	noble	ample
phase	tumble	high	elect
defect	castle	bundle	circle
tight	crackle	graph	enact

Story FP-13.1: "The Origin of Castles"

Section 2

Non-phonetic Word Recognition

Only read the real words in these paragraphs.

Dif stok nuroc answer dal ghomp rait
Father reps nusand librit people fgoyul
Ligeh woman dfopli fpoli wolen revery T
anc tlkop ipl answer ftyuop mploi

Wmoy answer vbca szxoc woman
Purst pim people Dagh duroc nare
Fwer father ncut marb goxe unlow
Qpiomt need women peris vgay

Jewsjht jjgk woman ohw kart lakh hlkar to
Woman people laugh jshetjkh jhjehre hkhsr
Sjherh heheh hehe hhrjhrakjhr khekha herp
Skejht skhetlsht selhelh lsehlkehslr hselkht

Answer to the kjsetlh kklhsetk hsalkhr jo
Site ak woman nskjteh during toto nerf
Sjkdhtht oiaeoit blood hiheta lugh sugar
Another Seth slktjehsklt lkshetlkshtl koet

jskherh ha thun sbtb there shah who
jhahr halhsrh lslkh klhslh a father kht
eshkjht eahsrh kslekht aeh answer
kja woman lkejtewsl would Leth

Story FP-13.1: "The Origin of Castles"   3 of 4

Section 3

Sentence Stacks

The difference between the castle

The difference between the castle and the prehistoric forts

The difference between the castle and the prehistoric forts was that castles

The difference between the castle and the prehistoric forts was that castles were established

The difference between the castle and the prehistoric forts was that castles were established as homes for nobles.

The great age

The great age of castle building

The great age of castle building started in Europe

The great age of castle building started in Europe by the Normans

The great age of castle building started in Europe by the Normans after the Saxons

The great age of castle building started in Europe by the Normans after the Saxons invaded England.

A moat

A moat was a point

A moat was a point of protection

A moat was a point of protection against invaders

A moat was a point of protection against invaders and helped to secure

A moat was a point of protection against invaders and helped to secure the inner constructs

A moat was a point of protection against invaders and helped to secure the inner constructs of the castle.

These castles

These castles had a strong

These castles had a strong stone tower

These castles had a strong stone tower called a keep

These castles had a strong stone tower called a keep where people lived.

The gate was

The gate was the entering point

The gate was the entering point to the castle

The gate was the entering point to the castle and at times

The gate was the entering point to the castle and at times it was enveloped

The gate was the entering point to the castle and at times it was enveloped by a shallow moat

The gate was the entering point to the castle and at times it was enveloped by a shallow moat that was filled

The gate was the entering point to the castle and at times it was enveloped by a shallow moat that was filled with water.

Story FP-13.1: "The Origin of Castles"

Section 4

Have you ever visited the United Kingdom and were impressed by the number of castles you could see? Castles can be found all around the world. The first castles ever built were just reinforced forts built for protection during wars and they look very different from the castles found around the world today. In much of Europe, castles were built in the middle ages. The difference between the castles and the prehistoric forts were that castles were established as homes for kings and other nobles who were extremely rich and important. The great age of castle building started in Europe by the Normans after the Saxons had invaded England. The first castles were built from wood and were called 'motte and bailey' castles. They were constructed on high piles of dirt and were very simple. However, these castles would catch fire easily. Later, castles were built out of stone and were much more durable. These castles had a strong stone tower called a 'keep' where people lived. The wall circling this tower was called a 'curtain wall'. The gate was the entering point to the castle and at times it was enveloped by a shallow moat that was filled with water. A moat was a point of protection against invaders. Today, you can view many different castles from all around the world and from different times. The one thing that will impress you is their grand size as well as their power.

Story FP-14.1: "Haichi – A Story of Love and Devotion"

Section 1

Isolated Phonogram Reading

ble	oa	gle	sp	ur
dr	ou	or	ea	ee
sw	squ	spl	oi	o
xt	onk	ai	oy	cl
mp	er	all	ir	pr

Nonsense Word Reading

rishow	drow	slead	kople	couse
drent	naist	flogrop	criswig	hilpmo
shroplup	crizz	drept	wixshromp	grustruse
squidmo	proxt	plofo	swetrum	clum
cridcrup	du	wedflom	vust	oatmeat

Real Word Reading

wait	choose	bronze	work
returning	adopt	greet	show
prevent	decided	eagerly	remains
master	station	unite	student
owner	former	while	away

Story FP-14.1: "Haichi – A Story of Love and Devotion"

Section 2

Non-phonetic Word Recognition

Only read the real words in these paragraphs.

Fgolst hwet during tblpo durat sulid
Chglop fhac sqwa friend ppoud nej
Bured Wald bumf enough fploi
Kelmfolt rough rkop aly lect tough

Phat friend minute gflop
Tqwest cdse Ort during
Bim sowas ldcfuit tough
Poud reb tay shlock faut

Jeljlkj tkljetlk minute kaerh al father alet
Jsf mother another kshfla who lkaetkh
Ksnfd jksdskj jsktn during slkte kjslrht
Minute kakjhe ajkhjminuter akhr hs to

Kjsrhtha ksrltej during peolep stskej
Enough jhseht through lkejt rough to
Another listep skjkehtkehtklh alkgeh
Lkjrtej kjf where ksjgtj lskjher here to

jsekjhr akejh hetkejh rhminute people to
ksjlth through Hlkset woman
should could rhijhrtj many kjslek both
kselkht should kjhtjkh sshjhralaskhjfakl busy

Story FP-14.1: "Haichi – A Story of Love and Devotion"

Section 3

Sentence Stacks

Every day when Professor Ueno

Every day when Professor Ueno went to work

Every day when Professor Ueno went to work in Tokyo

Every day when Professor Ueno went to work in Tokyo, Haichi would

Every day when Professor Ueno went to work in Tokyo, Haichi would accompany him

Every day when Professor Ueno went to work in Tokyo, Haichi would accompany him to the train station.

Many people travelled

Many people travelled to the station

Many people travelled to the station to be with Haichi

Many people travelled to the station to be with Haichi and feed him.

Legend has it

Legend has it that for the next ten years,

Legend has it that for the next ten years, Haichi would wait

Legend has it that for the next ten years, Haichi would wait at the train station

Legend has it that for the next ten years, Haichi would wait at the train station every day

Legend has it that for the next ten years, Haichi would wait at the train station every day for his master to return.

A former student

A former student of Professor Ueno

A former student of Professor Ueno discovered the dog's loyalty

A former student of Professor Ueno discovered the dog's loyalty for his master

A former student of Professor Ueno discovered the dog's loyalty for his master and sent a story

A former student of Professor Ueno discovered the dog's loyalty for his master and sent a story to the local newspaper.

It was destroyed

It was destroyed during World War

It was destroyed during World War Two but was rebuilt

It was destroyed during World War Two but was rebuilt in 1948

It was destroyed during World War Two but was rebuilt in 1948 where it still

It was destroyed during World War Two but was rebuilt in 1948 where it still remains today.

Story FP-14.1: "Haichi – A Story of Love and Devotion"

Section 4

Everyone loves a good tale about love, loyalty and dedication. This is the story of Haichi, a Japanese dog who loved his owner. Professor Ueno Eisabura decided he wanted to get a pet, so he decided on a specific dog: a Japanese Akita dog. He looked tirelessly for one, but instead he chose to adopt instead, thus choosing Haichi. Professor Ueno and Haichi did everything together and they were very close. Every day, when Professor Ueno went to work in Tokyo, Haichi would accompany him to the train station. Haichi would then wait patiently for his master to return so that he could get him. One day however, Professor Ueno didn't show up. Tragically, he had a stroke while at work and had passed away. However, this did not prevent Haichi from returning to the train station every day at 3pm eagerly awaiting the return of his master. Legend has it that for the next ten years, Haichi would wait at the train station every day for his master to return. A former student of Professor Ueno discovered the dog's loyalty for his master and sent a story to the local newspaper. Many people travelled to the station to be with Haichi and feed him and eventually a bronze statue was erected in Haichi's honour. It was destroyed during World War Two but was rebuilt in 1948 where it still remains today. The name Haichi means loyal in Japanese.

Story FP-15.1: "The Lost City of Atlantis – Fact or Fiction?"

Section 1

Isolated Phonogram Reading

ble	ea	oi	cle	y
dge	ft	er	g	ar
mp	tch	ou	mp	oy
ble	u-e	ow	o-e	aw
ph	sh	v	th	ch

Nonsense Word Reading

flixplu	twinrab	bry	spluflax	twixting
himplex	juxtrap	swigran	repted	kilped
spull	clume	traip	floub	vixray
swinrag	trixpot	lemprid	boraz	fingtrrab
splung	bufe	pru	extrimp	lingtrop

Real Word Reading

mythical	generation	peaceful	legend	back
society	evidence	magical	ancient	clock
mysterious	kilometre	civilization	research	jump
enthusiast	island	historical	answer	quid
kingdom	describe	scholar	castle	quack

Story FP-15.1: "The Lost City of Atlantis – Fact or Fiction?"

Section 2

Non-phonetic Word Recognition

Only read the real words in these paragraphs.

flam toodle flapdoodle though frixcro
juft gandriz felp island pordrip
huxt either trim braxter flo
squit nup period ponus

horb verig juv period wendix
neither grelps drind forv carping
rexed forn though inforp twen
melp wix blu neither wendrip

Period thorujhst sheag should skhtj lkjry
Neither lskhtk hseither ksdgkts either ti
Gksjetk lkjsekt jlkjwould whetlkh kjet to
From loath ks island laste kslktsetk who

Though lskejtkl j rough kjae people to
Lskejtl jl from ksrhth kh many naelkth
Periodi nesfrt should setlkh jslektj very
Skeet dfkl lktwo only snelkth l people

island through sthjh chark alkhr lkaehr
ahah either neither kntelkh ksdlkht two
island neither slkht hselkht skleh akhr ta
lkshtkh both should people skhtelht sake

Story FP-15.1: "The Lost City of Atlantis – Fact or Fiction?"

Section 3

Sentence Stacks

Many myths

Many myths and stories

Many myths and stories have been told

Many myths and stories have been told of the mythical

Many myths and stories have been told of the mythical city of Atlantis.

But scholars

But scholars have agreed

But scholars have agreed that there is

But scholars have agreed that there is no evidence

But scholars have agreed that there is no evidence that this magical city

But scholars have agreed that there is no evidence that this magical city ever existed.

This miracle find

This miracle find has left some

This miracle find has left some Atlantis legend enthusiasts

This miracle find has left some Atlantis legend enthusiasts to wonder

This miracle find has left some Atlantis legend enthusiasts to wonder if this could be

This miracle find has left some Atlantis legend enthusiasts to wonder if this could be the answer to

This miracle find has left some Atlantis legend enthusiasts to wonder if this could be the answer to the "Lost City".

They are calling

They are calling their find

They are calling their find a miracle

They are calling their find a miracle and have made

They are calling their find a miracle and have made a great deal

They are calling their find a miracle and have made a great deal of progress

They are calling their find a miracle and have made a great deal of progress in their research.

Perhaps the lost city

Perhaps the lost city of Atlantis

Perhaps the lost city of Atlantis will no longer be

Perhaps the lost city of Atlantis will no longer be a legend

Perhaps the lost city of Atlantis will no longer be a legend but a historical landmark

Perhaps the lost city of Atlantis will no longer be a legend but a historical landmark that we can learn

Perhaps the lost city of Atlantis will no longer be a legend but a historical landmark that we can learn about for years.

Story FP-15.1: "The Lost City of Atlantis – Fact or Fiction?"

Section 4

Many myths and stories have been told of the mythical city of Atlantis. The legend tells of a magical utopian society that was peaceful. The legend has captivated dreamers for generations, yet no one has found evidence of such a place in history books, or from any research. The city of Atlantis was first spoken about by Plato around 360 B.C. In his writings, he describes a very advanced and powerful society. But scholars have agreed that there is no evidence that this magical city ever existed. Or is there?

Recently, researchers from a university in Turkey have discovered the ancient remains of a 3000-year-old castle in the country's biggest lake, Lake Van. The mysterious castle, made of a special stone, spans about a kilometre with walls as high as four metres. Researchers believe it is an Iron Age relic of the lost Urartu Civilization or what is also known as the Kingdom of Van. They are calling their find a miracle and have made a great deal of progress in their research.

This miracle find has left some Atlantis legend enthusiasts to wonder if this could be the answer to the "Lost City". The mythical underwater island remains a legend for now but who knows? Perhaps this new castle discovery could hold answers for us. Perhaps the lost city of Atlantis will no longer be a legend but a historical landmark that we can learn about for years to come. Only time and research will tell.

Comprehension Plus!

Story CP-1.1: "Video Games – From Idea to Game"

Have you ever wondered how video games are created? Do you have a great idea for a game but are unsure of how to go about it? Creating video games is no simple task but if you approach it the right way, you just might have a chance at creating the next Minecraft.

Video games have been around since the early 1950s where they started off as research projects. In the late 60s video games started to become more sophisticated in their construction until the late 70s and early 80s when they blossomed with PAC Man, Space Invaders and Super Mario, until the super Play Station and Xboxes that we are familiar with today. These games were all created by large companies with large gaming teams in charge of creating the next big seller. Many people dream of creating the next big hit, but according to professional creators, you need to consider some important aspects when creating a game for others.

First, you need to do some research. According to the experts, you need to think of a game you love and think about why you love it and what specifically you love about it. This will help you realize and use the same "recipe" when creating your own game. You also need to consider games that you don't like and more importantly why you don't like them. What specifically do you not like – characters or genre – and make sure you remember this when creating your own game. Also, observe the games that others love to play and make sure you take into consideration everyone's views as you don't want to create a game with narrow market appeal.

Next, pick a niche or a genre and stick to it. For example, if you are going to choose the theme of sci-fi make sure that your game uses these elements and doesn't go too far off the beaten track. Use traditional elements found within these genres but feel free to be creative. Your game needs to be creative and somewhat believable for people to be interested in it. Don't use every element as it might make the game hard to follow and too difficult to play. Most professional experts would agree that if your game is overly complex and complicated, it risks isolating and turning off potential game players.

Finally, do the preparation and leg work. Make sure the game has easy to follow instructions and rules.

Make sure they are consistent to the type of game you want to design and make sure it has something unique and different to catch the eye of potential gamers. Know that you are doing this to come up with lots of ideas but realize that not all of them will work and you will need to streamline your final product.

You can always opt to go independently or you can approach a company once you are done, but either way, it's a competitive industry. Remember the idea is just the first important step, but know that many of the games you love and play today started as a great idea first.

Story CP-2.1: "Viola Desmond – A Canadian Legacy"

On a chilly winter's night in 1946, Viola Desmond, an African-Canadian hair salon owner, went to see a movie at the Roseland Theatre in New Glasgow, Nova Scotia. What started out as a nice night out, ended up being a miserable night in prison for Viola. As she took her seat on the main floor of the theatre, Viola did not know that the Roseland Theatre was racially segregated. Ms. Viola was a black woman and black patrons, at the time, were only allowed to sit in the balcony seats. Ms. Desmond was told to move from her seat and she refused, determined to be treated as an equal. Viola Desmond was subsequently arrested and dragged out of the theatre.

Viola Desmond was no stranger to being faced with inequality. She knew what it meant to work and strive for things that she wanted even though people said that she couldn't. Viola grew up in Nova Scotia, dreaming of becoming a beautician and hairdresser and to run her own beauty salon. Learning that beauty schools in Nova Scotia did not accept black students, she decided to get trained in Montreal and the United States and then she promptly moved back to her home province and opened up her own beauty salon.

Viola Desmond knew what it was like to fight for what she wanted, so when she faced being sent to prison for sitting in a seat in a movie theatre, she decided to fight for her rights. She took the fight all the way to the Supreme Court and fought to end racial segregation in Canada. Unfortunately, Ms. Desmond's court battles did not end well and her appeal was denied. Ms. Desmond's fight took a big toll on her personal life leaving her with a broken marriage, an abandoned business and a premature death in 1965.

Viola Desmond's fight against racism and inequality did not go unnoticed, however. In 2010, Ms. Desmond's cause was officially recognized by the Lieutenant Governor of Nova Scotia and she was pardoned. In 2018, Viola Desmond was nationally recognized by having her face appear on a Canadian postage stamp and the new $10 bill.

Viola Desmond's story of strength, determination and courage is one that we can look to for inspiration to fight for what is right and to never give up. Who would have thought that a night out at the movies would turn into an inspiring Canadian civil rights legacy?

Story CP-3.1: "Gum! Chew on the History!"

Chewing gum has been around for thousands of years but many people are unaware of its original form and history. The very first form of chewing gum was discovered by Mayans and Aztecs in the form of *chicle:* a resin extracted from the sapodilla tree in Mexico and Latin America. *Chicle* is a strong resin that acts similarly to a band-aid for trees. It is a sticky, rubber substance that is meant to protect tree bark, but Mayans and Aztecs discovered that it could also be chewable if sliced thinly and cooked and dried out. This first form of "cha" helped to ward off hunger and thirst but the Aztec's also recognized it as a powerful breath freshener. European settlers quickly picked up and capitalized on this habit of chewing "cha" from the Native American cultures and soon it became popular in America as well.

Inventor Thomas Adams Sr. received a supply of chicle through a Mexican president and originally thought it would be a helpful industrial substance because of its plastic-like qualities. However, he soon learned that once boiled and hand rolled, it would be more popular as pieces of chewing gum. By the late 1800s Adams gum was widely sold. Around the same time, a soap salesman named William Wrigley came up with a smart idea to sell soap. He would give out free gum to customers who bought the most soap! When he realized that the gum was more popular than the soap, he decided to switch careers. After much trial and error, the William Wrigley Jr. Company took off and by the time Wrigley died in 1932, he was one of the richest men in America.

As the demand for gum grew in places like America, the cost to natural resources in Latin America began to take its toll. Soon the demand for chicle outmatched the resource (the sapodilla trees) and gum manufactures began switching to cheaper synthetic bases made from petroleum, wax and other substances. By 1980, The United States was no longer importing chicle from Mexico or other Latin American countries.

So, what's the difference between chewing gum and bubble gum? Bubble gum is made to be extra stretchy, so that you can blow bubbles with it. Frank Fleer invented bubble gum in 1906 and called it Blibber Blubber, but it didn't really become popular until 1928 when Walter Diemer first developed the Double Bubble that is so famous today. What's the secret to blowing the perfect bubble? The warmth in your mouth softens the gum creating a base. Chewing separates the sugar and the colouring and helps to align the long molecules in the gum base, which can then be stretched easier than with chewing gum. To blow great bubbles you are supposed to chew until all the flavour is gone so that the sugar molecules don't weaken the bubble. Gum bases don't react to your mouth or stomach lining, so if you swallow it accidentally, don't worry, it won't get stuck!

    Clark, J & McIntosh, M. (2022) *Just Read* © Pavilion Publishing and Media Ltd 2022.

Story CP-4.1: "Brain signals, Body Screens and Brain Implants! Oh My!"

Imagine you are sitting at home thinking about asking your friend to go see a movie with you. Without picking up a phone, your thoughts are sent directly from your brain to your friend's brain. Your friend sends a "brain message" back to you telling you that they'll meet you there at 6pm. Crazy, right? Not really. That is one of the many new ways that scientists are predicting that we will communicate in the near future. Human communication has come a long way.

The way humans communicate has transformed a great deal since the first man walked the earth. The origin of speech can be traced back to 500,000 BC. From solely relying on the spoken word, man moved into communicating in written form using symbols and carvings into rock surfaces. By 9000 BC, man had developed pictograms or symbols representing concepts of activities or objects. The first alphabet came into existence in 2000 BC. From there, we had many ways of communicating such as storytelling, written words on paper, and the use of quills for writing. The first telephone was invented in 1876 revolutionizing the way humans communicate from far distances. And, believe it or not, the first mobile phone was created in 1947! From there, the development of computers and the internet happened and since then, the way we communicate has been changing at lightning speed. Now, it's almost unheard of to see someone who doesn't have a mobile phone. Telephone booths are becoming relics of the past and almost nobody understands having to use a dial to make a phone call.

But what will happen from here? It's almost impossible to think that communication can get any easier. With the touch of a screen, we can make plans to go out, make emergency calls, send pictures of ourselves and call in sick for work. We don't even have to actually speak to people anymore, we can do it all by sending text messages or emails. But scientists are now saying that we can look forward to getting implants in our bodies that allow us to have wearable screens on our skin or our clothing. Goodbye, mobile phone, hello, screen on my forearm! Scientists are also researching and testing something called "Brain-Computer Interfaces". These can literally allow us to send our thoughts to someone else through a special network; no phone, no computer, no screen… just our brains; amazing and scary!

There's no question that we are now living in a fast-paced world with ways of communicating that are so easy and quick. It's hard to imagine, but get ready for the day we no longer use phones but we use our brains and bodies to speak to one another.

Story CP-5.1: "The Amazing Wayne Gretzy"

"You miss 100 percent of the shots you don't take" Wayne Gretzky

He has smashed national hockey records in all categories, coached various NHL hockey teams, owned a chain of restaurants and was the youngest athlete signed to a team in the history of American sports. The amazing Wayne Gretzky has done it all. His path to stardom was paved with hard work, unrelenting determination and amazing skill.

Born January 26, 1961, in Brantford Ontario, Wayne Gretzky started skating before the age of three under the guidance of his father, Walter Gretzky. He mastered the art of hockey in his backyard hockey rink and started playing minor hockey at the age of six. Debuting on the Nadrofsky Steelers, Wayne Gretzky played hockey with players four years his senior. In his 1970-71 season, Gretzky scored 196 goals and 120 assists. This amazing start soon pegged him as a young hockey prodigy whose future held great promise. In 1975, Gretzky moved to Toronto and began playing Junior B hockey. He first played with the Vaughn Nationals and in '76-'77 moved to the Seneca Nationals. In 1977-78 he began playing full time in OHL (Ontario Hockey League) with the Sault Saint Marie Greyhounds. In his inaugural season he earned the rookie record with 70 goals and 112 assists in 64 games. It was with the Sault Saint Marie Greyhounds that he first donned the number 99, and Wayne Gretzky would soon become a household sensation.

In 1978, Gretzky turned professional and would be the youngest professional athlete playing a major league sport in America. His first professional team was with the Indianapolis Racers with whom he only played eight games before being traded to the Edmonton Oilers. By the start of Gretzky's second season, the WHA had merged with the NHL and it wasn't long before Gretzky ruled this league. With his time spent with the Edmonton Oilers, Gretzky began shattering hockey records. Some of these included most goals scored, most assists, and the most points in a season. Gretzky also led the Oilers to four Stanley Cup championships before being traded to the LA Kings in 1988. Unable to recapture the magic he had with the Oilers, Gretzky added greatly to the profile of the LA Kings and hockey in the Southwest US. After a quick stint with the St. Louis Blues, Gretzky was traded to the New York Rangers where he finished his hockey career.

Wayne Gretzky retired from the Rangers after playing three seasons at the age of 38. At his last hockey game, The NHL retired the number 99 in recognition of Wayne Gretzky's contribution to the world of hockey.

After his hockey career, Gretzky became involved with coaching for the NHL and for International and Olympic hockey teams. He coached the Phoenix Coyotes for five years and left to start up new business ventures. Mixing his love of hockey with business, Wayne Gretzky became a successful entrepreneur and owned ventures such as a winery, a chain of restaurants as well as ownership of the CFL team the Toronto Argonauts. Gretzky was inducted into the Hockey Hall of fame on June 23, 1999. In 2016, the NHL appointed him the official ambassador for the league's celebrations in 2017.

Living with his family in Southern California, Gretzky will always be remembered as the "great one". His style, his game and his sense of modesty are inspirations to those who aspire to be great hockey players.

Story CP-6.1: "Terry's Marathon Journey"

In schools all across Canada, students participate in an annual run named after an amazing man called Terry Fox. Who was Terry Fox and why do children across Canada honour his memory every year by running a race and raising money?

Terry Stanley Fox was born in Winnipeg, Manitoba, and lived in Port Coquitlam, BC. Terry was an active boy participating in many sporting activities. Unfortunately, when Terry Fox was 18-years-old, he found out that he had bone cancer. Terry had to have his right leg amputated just above the knee. While he was in hospital being treated for his cancer, he witnessed many other people suffering from the disease and he was strongly affected by the sight. Seeing children suffering, in particular, bothered Terry immensely. So much so that he decided that he would begin a run across Canada to raise money for Cancer research. He would call the run the "Marathon of Hope".

It took Terry Fox 18 months to prepare for the "Marathon of Hope"; with one leg amputated, and using a prosthetic leg, he ran 5,000 kilometers to get himself ready. He started his run across the country in St. John's, Newfoundland. He ran close to 42 kilometers a day throughout the Atlantic provinces and the East Coast.

The country's attention grew and grew as he persevered and ran with the hope of raising money for cancer research. After 143 days and 5,373 kilometers, Terry Fox woke up one day and discovered he had a nasty cough which indicated that he cancer in his lungs. Sadly, Terry Fox had to stop his run without achieving his dream. Terry Fox passed away at the age of 22 on June 28, 1981.

However, Terry Fox's story does not end there. His legacy lives on today and to date, 750 million dollars has been raised in his name through the annual Terry Fox run. You may have even participated in a Terry Fox run in your school. The story of Terry Fox is a sad one but it is also full of inspiration and hope; hope that we can find a cure for cancer but also hope that we can look to him as a source of inspiration. Terry Fox has shown us that compassion and determination can create lasting change. All over Canada, statues of Terry Fox have been erected. His memory and his legacy will live on in the history of Canada.

Story CP-7.1: "The Story of Bill Reid – Artist Extraordinaire"

Bill Reid is Canada's most renowned contemporary Native Northwest Coast artist. His work spans many mediums – goldsmithing, sculpting and writing. He is an example of a native artist whose calling was to bring Northwest Haida art back from the brink of extinction, but his path was an unusual one.

Born in Victoria, BC, on January 12, 1920, he was an only child. Bill Reid's mother was of Haida ancestry although Bill would not embrace his Haida roots until later in his life. Bill Reid grew up in British Columbia and it wasn't until a family trip in his mid-twenties to his mother's village that he came in contact with his artistic roots and his sense of Haida belonging. It was during his 1954 visit that Bill Reid saw family members wearing intricate bracelets designed by his great-great Uncle Charles Edenshaw and this sparked his life-long love of art and Haida culture.

At the start of his career, the young Bill Reid was first employed by the CBC as a broadcaster for a late night radio show. Later, Bill Reid studied jewelry making in the 1950s at Ryerson Polytechnical Institute and then attended the London School of Design to learn classical European techniques. Returning back to BC, Reid opened his own studio while still working for the CBC. In the late 60s, Reid had an opportunity to work for British Columbia's Museum of Anthropology resurrecting traditional Haida totem poles. The project was an attempt to preserve many traditional forms of Haida Gwaii art that were in danger of being lost. From here, Reid's life-long interest in using traditional Haida Gwaii figures and characters to make his art blossomed. His most famous pieces are representations from famous Haida Gwaii stories and are recognized around the world today as pieces distinctly representing Native Canadian Northwest Coastal art. One of his most famous sculptures, The Raven and the First Men, is on display at UBC's Museum of Anthropology and it depicts the human creation story according to Haida legend. Another of Reid's most recognizable sculptures can be found in Vancouver International Airport. Originally commissioned for the Canadian Embassy in Washington, The Spirit of the Haida Gwaii is an argillite carving depicting miniature canoes and draws from the oral histories of the Haida. In 2004, a replica of this stunning piece was added to the Canadian Twenty Dollar bill in order to celebrate Canada's history and achievements.

As a writer, a carver, a jeweller maker and story teller, Bill Reid's art has touched and inspired many great Native and non-Native Canadian artists. There's not a person in Northwest Coast Art who hasn't been touched by Reid's interpretation of Haida Art. The Bill Reid Gallery was opened in Vancouver in 2008 to celebrate the story and contribution of one of Canada's greatest modern artists.

Story CP-8.1: "Your Amazing Brain"

Have you ever thought about your brain? If you have, you will have used your brain to think about your brain! How amazing is that? Your brain is an incredible and very necessary part of your body. Your brain is an organ contained inside of your head. It has some super important jobs like making you think, remember, see, hear, touch, feel and move. Your brain weighs about three pounds and it is made up of cells and tissue. The brain has two parts to it; the left side or **hemisphere**, and the right side or **hemisphere**. If you were to look at your brain, it kind of looks like a ball of macaroni but it is so much more than that and chances are that it wouldn't taste that great either!

Your brain has many parts that have very different jobs. The **cerebrum** helps you to think and speak. So, when you are chatting with your friend about your cool new bike trick, you are using your **cerebrum**. The **cerebellum** helps you with movement and balance. As you are running out to the soccer field ready to play your game and score some goals, your **cerebellum** is hard at work helping you to move on the field and to keep your balance as you kick the ball. The **prefrontal cortex** helps you to make plans and decisions. It's funny to think about what the **prefrontal cortex** was doing when you decided to eat that jalapeno! The **hippocampus** has nothing to do with hippos being in your brain, rather it is the part of your brain that finds and stores memories. Remember when you lost your first tooth? You're now using your **hippocampus!** The **amygdala** has the important job of controlling your emotions. Ever felt scared to go into a dark room? Your **amygdala** is doing its job of alerting you and keeping you safe by triggering different emotions in you. Finally, connecting all of these parts are **neurons** which are amazing cells that make electrical signals to send messages to other cells in your body telling them what to do. The brain is one busy organ!

What's even more cool about the brain is that you can do things to help make it stronger. Learning new things helps your brain stretch and get stronger and the more you learn, your brain gets stronger and stronger. Now, almost everyone thinks that making mistakes is a bad thing but, guess what? Making mistakes is an even more powerful way to make your brain grow and get stronger.

So, the next time you do, well, anything, use your brain to think about how amazing your brain really is!

    Clark, J & McIntosh, M. (2022) *Just Read* © Pavilion Publishing and Media Ltd 2022.

Story CP-9.1: "How Dogs Communicate"

Have you ever wondered how man's best friend can understand you, or better yet, how you can understand your dog? Dogs communicate very differently than humans but it's still easy to understand the intent of the message. When dogs communicate with other dogs they do so in a very different manner. While dogs are able to hear the difference between different types of barks, they also rely on smell and other senses to figure out the message from another dog. From a smell, a dog can determine the status of a dog, if they are male or female or if they are dominate or submissive.

When communicating with people, dogs use a different style of communication. Depending on your dog's need, they use body signals to tell you their intentions. One of the most obvious forms of body language is observation or using those big sad eyes. Dogs will often use their gaze to infer their needs to their owners. In a term called inferential gazing, dogs are able to infer their need for food, walks and attention. There is no need for barking or paw gestures, they merely use gazing as a way to show you what they need. This is very similar to the way an infant communicates its needs to his/her mother. When humans are communicating with dogs, alternating the gaze between object and or direction, a dog will be able to infer (guess) that you are interested in a "thing" in that direction. This type of messaging is particularly effective if the human talks to the dog first and then gazes in the direction that holds the object. The dog will then infer that the command and the direction is directly linked to what you are trying to convey.

Another way in which dogs communicate with humans is through body language. If you are watching carefully and can read the signals, it's actually quite easy to gauge your dog's intentions. Scientists have identified 19 gestures dogs most commonly use to communicate with humans. Direct and open eye contact is a dog's way of showing you trust and affection while avoiding eye contact is a signal that the dog may be scared or has done something wrong. Tail posture is another indication of a dog's mood or temperament. If a dog's tail is wagging slowly, this is a signal that the dog is unsure or weary. A stiff tail means an alert state while a tucked tail indicates feeling scared. Of course, a waggy tail is used to convey happiness and a low tail can mean contentedness or feeling good. Tongue licking, yawning or misplaced sneezing can all be signs that your dog is anxious, stressed or nervous. Yawning can be tricky because it can also be interpreted as feeling relaxed, so it's important to think of your dog's mood when he/she yawns.

Belly exposure is also a way of telling a person how the dog is feeling. Dogs usually show their bellies to humans as a way of trying to appease a person or seek attention. A belly rub is a good way for a human and dog to share affection and build their trust. If a dog suddenly greets you with a downward dog, this is his/her way of initiating play. If you respond with a downward dog back, this will engage your dog in play as it tells him/her that you are reading them and want to play as well. Pawing or raising a paw, is a way to catch a human's attention and then further signal their intention with a gaze.

Humans and dogs have had a long history of co-existence and share a unique bond. Together, dogs and humans are able to support one another and offer each other unconditional support. The key to good communication between us is being able to read the signals and understand that communication doesn't have to be complicated.

Story CP-10.1: "Learning Disability or Super Power?"

What is a learning disability? A learning disability is what can happen when a person's brain is "wired" differently. A learning disability can't be cured or fixed, rather it is something that a person lives with for their whole lives. When someone has a learning disability, they might struggle with reading, writing, math or keeping and holding attention or focus. There are many different learning disabilities that people can be diagnosed with. Did you know that there are many famous people, celebrities and billionaires alike, who live with learning disabilities? It's hard to tell when someone has a learning disability because you can't see it on the outside, so it might come as a surprise to you that many very successful people in the world live with different learning challenges like dyslexia, autism, attention deficit disorder and many more. In fact, the list of successful and famous people living with learning challenges is so long, it would take forever to talk about them all. So, let's talk about just a few of these amazing folks who have overcome their difficulties and have learned to live with and sometimes even use their differences to help them succeed.

Being a professional or Olympic athlete can be tough. The number of hours of practice it takes to master a sport is astronomical, not to mention the perseverance and drive that it takes to become the best at a chosen sport. There are many athletes who have had the additional challenge of having a learning disability. Michael Phelps, the most decorated Olympian of all time, talks openly about learning to live with Attention Deficit Hyperactivity Disorder (ADHD). Michael experienced many struggles along the way. One of his teachers even told him that he would never succeed at anything. Despite Michael having ADHD, he pushed through and used his diagnosis to help him become one of the best Olympic swimmers in the world.

Many famous actors including Tom Cruise and Channing Tatum live with dyslexia and overcame their challenges to become very successful actors in their field. Many business leaders, artists, musicians and thought leaders also have achieved an amazing amount of success and fame despite – or perhaps even because of – their learning challenges. The famous artist Pablo Picasso struggled a great deal in school and, in fact, failed due to his reading difficulties.

So, it just goes to show you that just because someone has a disability, doesn't mean that they can't do something they love or be successful in anything. Having a learning disability just means that you have to learn how you learn best and try to find teachers and support people who can teach you how you need to learn. It's also about understanding your own personal learning differences and persevering through the hard times. While it may take someone with a learning disability a bit longer to do something, who knows, they just might come up with a whole new way to do that thing and become successful and famous in the process!

 Clark, J & McIntosh, M. (2022) *Just Read* © Pavilion Publishing and Media Ltd 2022.

Story CP-11.1: "Edinburgh Castle"

What famous castle housed royalty, was a garrison and held a leading military presence throughout history? The answer is Edinburgh Castle. This famous castle boasts inhabitants from the Bronze age (850 BCE) who built a hill fort on what is now known as Castle Rock. What makes Edinburgh Castle so fascinating and impressive is its numerous reincarnations and breathtaking views of Edinburgh itself.

Historically, many royals have lived in this castle. The first King of Scotland, Malcom III Canmore, made the castle his residence between 1058-1093. The city's oldest and smallest chapel is located in the castle and was made in honour of Malcom's wife, Margaret. Also of note, Mary Queen of Scots resided in the castle and gave birth to her son James, who would later become the Scottish and English King who unified the crowns of Scotland and England in 1603. The last known monarch to reside within the castle was Charles I in 1633, who lived there before his coronation as King of Scots.

Given the frequency and outbreak of war, Edinburgh Castle was also used as a strategic military post. Many times, the castle changed hands between the Scottish and the English and it was also used as a garrison that held many prisoners of war throughout history. Between the years of 1757 to 1814, the castle housed prisoners from the Seven Years War, The American Revolution and the Napoleonic Wars. During World War Two, German aircraft Luftwaffe pilots who were shot down in battle were housed in the infirmary within the castle. Today, there are many reminders of the castle's military history. One of the oldest and largest canons resides at Edinburgh Castle. Named Mon's Meg, this cannon was given as a gift in 1457 to James II and weighs six-tonnes and could fire a 150kg gunstone for up to 3.2km (2 miles). In honour of Mary Queen of Scot's wedding, Mon let out a blast that is reported to have gone from the Castle to Royal Botanical Gardens!

The castle's rich history and elaborate construction can be viewed today. Many of Scotland's treasures can be found within its walls. The Scot's Crown Jewels are located here as well as the famous Stone of Destiny, which was returned to Scotland in 1996. The place also hosts some great rooms inside such as The Great Hall, a room which saw many famous kings and queens plan their futures as important historical rulers.

Today, Edinburgh Castle is a historical site that houses The Scottish War Memorial Museum and the castle itself became a UNESCO world heritage site in 1995. Located 443 feet above sea level, you can see many other famous Edinburgh treasures such as the Scot Monument, Waverly Train Station and Arthur's Seat – a series of braes and crags to the west of the city. Visited by over one million tourists each year, Edinburgh Castle is a favourite of historians, architects and military enthusiasts who appreciate the vast historical importance of this ancient building. Planning a trip to Edinburgh? Make sure to arrange a visit to this beloved and fascinating piece of Scottish history.

    Clark, J & McIntosh, M. (2022) *Just Read* © Pavilion Publishing and Media Ltd 2022.

Story CP-12.1: "The Truth About Pirates"

What do you imagine when you think of a pirate? You might picture a dirty, evil-looking sailor with a patch on one eye, a wooden leg and a sword in his hand. There are many stories and movies about pirates and some of these stories make pirates out to be funny or heroes of a sort. The truth is that pirates were robbers and they were extremely ruthless and would commit almost any crime to get what they wanted.

Piracy began over 2000 years ago in Ancient Greece when these robbers of the sea would raid ships along the trading routes. The pirates would jump onto ships and loot and steal anything they wanted and if anyone got in their way, they wouldn't hesitate to hurt or even kill people. In truth, these men were merciless and evil bandits. It's curious that the movies would glorify such a horrible type of person.

Piracy was at its peak for about one hundred years, from 1620 to 1720. It was during those years that people rarely felt safe when out at sea. Ultimately, most pirates were always searching for ways to get rich and to give themselves a better life. Often pirates were heavily armed and they would always find new and clever ways to get what they wanted. Pirates were often very superstitious and had some very strange beliefs when they were out at sea. Pirates believed that wearing pierced earrings would save their eyesight. They also believed that having a woman on board their ship was very bad luck. As such, women had to disguise themselves as men to board any pirate ship.

Surprisingly, there was such a thing as a legal pirate. The government recognized the power of pirates and found a way to hire them as "privateers". These privateers were allowed to attack and plunder enemy ships and then share their loot with the government.

There were many famous pirates to sail the seas and to this day, there are still men who attack ships at sea but these are very few and they often are swiftly captured and punished. While the movies show us the shiny side of piracy, it's good to remember that these people were not only robbers of the sea but greedy and ruthless lawbreakers.

    Clark, J & McIntosh, M. (2022) *Just Read* © Pavilion Publishing and Media Ltd 2022.

Story CP-13.1: "The Guinness Book of World Records"

Who has the longest beard? Who has the record of being the tallest man ever? All of these plus more can be found in *The Guinness Book of World Records*. This book keeps track of information and records established around the world and many meaningful and sometimes bizarre facts.

The Guinness Book of World Records was first published on August 27, 1955, and came about as a result of an odd argument. The story began at a hunting party in Ireland in 1951, when the managing director of Guinness Brewing company, Sir Hugh Beaver, found himself in an argument about whether or not the golden plover was Europe's fastest game bird. He wanted to know if this was true and looked for a book that would give an authoritative answer, but he could not find one. He thought it would be a good idea if someone came up with such a book and decided to remedy this. At the time, someone working at the Guinness Brewing company put Sir Hugh Beaver in touch with the twin brothers Norris and Ross McWhirter, who were running a publishing and fact-finding company in London. These two brothers had an amazing ability to memorize fact and figures and recall them immediately and accurately. Guinness was so impressed by their amazing skills that he commissioned the twins to start a book. *The Guinness Book of World Records* was soon born. The McWhirters were the editors, compilers and spirit behind the book. In 1972, these amazing brothers could be found on TV, on the show Roy Castle's

'Record Breakers', impressing viewers with their ability to reproduce facts and figures on the spot. Unfortunately, Ross McWhirter was shot dead in 1975. Norris continued as editor until 1986 and later retired in 1996.

The Guinness Book of World Records is well loved around the world by adults and children alike for meticulous accuracy and amazing breadth of subjects and, let's be honest, its weird facts! All world records are solemnly checked and authenticated and new records are encouraged, but how does one go about establishing a world record?

In order to get into The Guinness Book of World Records, you must meet some criteria or standards. The criteria and standards are carefully outlined on their website but the important thing to remember about these standards is that the records must be able to be measured objectively (by a number or amount), that it must be easily reproduced, that it does not harm anyone or anything, nor can it break the law. It is a rigorous application process and admission requirements are strict, but both individuals and small groups are always encouraged to set new records and achieve their best.

Today, The Guinness Book of World Records still continues to be a best seller. It has sold over a hundred million copies and has been translated to 23 languages in over 100 different countries. Ever dreamed of breaking or establishing a new world record? Check out Guinness' website and let the games begin!

Story CP-14.1: "Black Holes"

Have you ever wondered what outer space feels like? We know it is a collection of stars, planets and galaxies, but what about other possibilities? A point of fascination to both scientists and other people is the idea of black holes. We know of their existence, but what exactly is a black hole and how did they come to be? What can we learn from studying them and what future possibilities can black holes hold?

A black hole is a cosmic body of extremely intense gravity from which nothing, not even light, can escape. A black hole can be formed by the death of a massive star. Black holes are so strong that anything that comes close to them disappears because of their intense gravitational force or pull. Albert Einstein first predicted the existence or possibilities of black holes in 1916 with his general theory of relativity. Later, the term black hole was born in 1967 by American astronomer John Wheeler and the existence of the very first black hole was discovered in 1971.

Black holes are extreme gravity forces, but are all black holes created equally? There are three main types of black holes: stellar black holes, supermassive black holes, and intermediate black holes. Stellar black holes are the smallest of the subtypes of black holes. A stellar black hole is created when a large star collapses in on itself and continues to compress. This dead star, or newly formed black hole, is incredibly dense, which gives it a huge gravitational force. This gravitational force then allows it to capture dust and gas and other matter, and it becomes denser and denser, increasing its gravitational force and overall strength.

Supermassive black holes, similar to stellar black holes, are built in the same fashion but their power and force is a billion times more massive than the sun. Scientists think that supermassive black holes may have been formed by thousands of tiny black holes merging together. Because black holes consume and grow from gathering the dust and space material around them, as they consume more, they grow and become more massive and powerful. Thus, a cycle is established and the super massive "giants" continue to grow and build throughout the galaxy.

Intermediate black holes are thought to be somewhere between stellar black holes and supermassive black holes in size and mass. Intermediate black holes are thought to form when stars in a cluster collide and form a chain reaction. Their construction is similar to that of the supermassive black holes but on a lesser scale.

Because black holes are unseen, how do we know they exist? The answer lies in the gravitational field that surrounds these invisible gems. Black holes are detected by the amount of gravitational force that scientists encounter in space. Try to imagine an invisible force that continues to suck in space objects such a dust and gas but never allows anything out. Imagine the amount of heat, radiation and gravity that these massive objects produces. This is what allows scientists to detect the existence of a black hole. Scientists believe that studying black holes is useful because they are a useful tool for discovering fundamental laws about our universe. Scientists believe that by studying black holes we will be able to rethink big picture ideas such as matter, and apply new ideas to the study of physics. Studying black holes may also help people to gain a better understanding as to the nature and the origins of our universe.

   Clark, J & McIntosh, M. (2022) *Just Read* © Pavilion Publishing and Media Ltd 2022.